spring 2014

16:1

ƒOURTH GENRE

EXPLORATIONS IN NONFICTION

Fourth Genre: Explorations in Nonfiction (ISSN 1522-3868) is published twice a year (Spring, Fall) by Michigan State University Press with support from the Michigan State University College of Arts and Letters and Department of Writing, Rhetoric, & American Cultures.

BUSINESS OFFICE

Subscriptions, orders, renewals, change of address, claims for missing issues: Michigan State University Press Journals; PO Box 121; Congers, NY 10920-0121; TEL (845) 267-3054; FAX (845) 267-3478; EMAIL *msupjournals@cambeywest. com*. *All other inquiries:* Michigan State University Press Journals, 1405 S. Harrison Rd., Ste. 25; East Lansing, MI 48823-5245; TEL (517) 884-6914; FAX (517) 432-2611; EMAIL *journals@msu.edu*; WEB *www.msupress.org/journals/fg*.

Send manuscripts to editorial office only; do not send manuscripts to MSU Press.

SUBSCRIPTION RATES (1 YEAR / 2 ISSUES)

Current subscription rates and ordering options are available at *www.msupress.org/journals*.

PREPAYMENT REQUIRED: Check, money order, Visa, and MasterCard accepted. Make checks payable to Michigan State University Press. Payment must be in U.S. currency drawn from a U.S. bank.

RETURN, CREDIT, REFUND, AND CLAIMS POLICY

Returns are not accepted. MSU Press Journals Division can provide full or partial credit only for subscription orders. Credits issued for cancellations will be pro-rated. Credit can be transferred only to other MSU Press journals, not to MSU Press book products. Pending subscriptions can be refunded in full. Allow 8–12 weeks for processing. Domestic claims must be received within 3 months of publication date. International claims must be received within 6 months of publication date.

SINGLE COPIES, BACK ISSUES, AND REPRINTS

To ORDER REPRINTS OF PREVIOUS VOLUMES, CONTACT: Periodicals Service, Inc., 11 Main St.; Germantown, NY 12526; (518) 537-4700; *psc@periodicals.com*; *www.periodicals.com/html/ihp_e.html?ef64353*.

Fourth Genre is indexed or abstracted in: Current Abstracts, IBR Literary Reference Center, Literature Online (LION), Periodical Abstracts, ProQuest, Scopus, Ulrichsweb.

Fourth Genre participates in Project MUSE®, a Johns Hopkins University initiative that provides online institutional access to leading scholarly publications in the arts, humanities, and social sciences at *http://muse.jhu.edu*.

g green press INITIATIVE Michigan State University Press is a member of the Green Press Initiative and is committed to developing and encouraging ecologically responsible publishing practices. For more information about the Green Press Initiative and the use of recycled paper in book publishing, please visit *www.greenpressinitiative. org*. This journal was printed on FSC certified paper.

CONTENTS

EDITOR'S NOTE

LEAVING A TRACE

"What was he *thinking?*"

I am sitting across from my father's tax adviser as she pours over some of the papers I've been sorting for the past four months. She is asking the same question I find myself voicing aloud periodically when I just can't make sense of his filing system, or the beneficiary he named on one of his accounts, or the big gap in record-keeping, or his file-naming habits.

"He was so careful about all these matters, so attentive to details . . . why would he have left it like this?" she asks, and has no better answer than I do, no way other than speculating what might have led my father to do or not do one thing rather than another. We can no longer consult him.

We are trying to sort through his papers, settle accounts, trying to make sure everything is in place to provide my mother with what is needed, to keep her bills paid in a way that relieves her of worry. Everything will, eventually, be fine, I know; everything will settle into place and start running in a (different) kind of routine.

In the days after the funeral, after all the people had gone home, I sat at his desk—handmade from the heaviest light oak he could afford, massive and dense—with the two file drawers open, one on each side of the computer. I sat there trying to figure out where the important papers were, what kinds of things went on which side, which were active files that I needed to make phone calls about first and which were merely records of old accounts. I tried to understand his logic, his thinking.

Eventually I found that in order to make sense of it—so that I could begin to work through each task systematically—I would have to re-label files and order them differently. But for weeks I was loathe to make any changes. Here, after all, was how he had arranged them, and it must have created a picture for him, a kind of sense. No doubt another person would have gone about this differently. But I'm a person who reads, who looks at the arrangement of matter trying to discern a sense-making logic, and so I have spent far too long trying to read my father in his file labels and in the arrangement of his papers and records, trying to conjure him back in this way.

What was he thinking about?

How to make his social security check, the pension he received, and bits and pieces of investments he'd made over time yield sufficiently to take care of my mother. How to give instructions to his grown children that would sustain them, how to get them to do what he wished they'd do without him. He was dealing with regrets. He was enjoying himself, too—with the way email gave him an opportunity to stay in touch with people from his work life, his religious life, his community life. He bought U.S. Mint coins in proof sets. He listened to the catalog of Frank Sinatra albums that he'd managed to upload to the computer. He talked daily to my brother and tried not to dwell on his disappointment at not being able to watch his grandsons play football in person. He tried, too, not to dwell on what ached or didn't work right, but more and more in the written record he left, you can see it interrupting the care he usually took—even with his two-fingered typing—to get things right.

I know a lot about what he was paying attention to, but not what he made of it all. I also know it's a privilege to have this text to struggle with. He wasn't a writer, nor very well-read, but he did at times put words to paper when he wanted to be sure we knew what mattered to him, what moved him. Now that he is no longer here, I look to the traces of himself that he left, in the words he sent, in the things he collected as well as the things he discarded, in his arrangement of his file drawers and his hard drive.

I have been thinking of all this as I re-encounter the essays that fill this issue of *Fourth Genre* as it goes to press, because I find an affinity to so many of them, to each writer. So much that goes unspoken, so much in them about the attempt to decode or read a story. Sheryl St. Germain trying to read herself into the mass she attends for her friend's dead son. Kathryn Winograd trying to read climatological changes in the leavings of a packrat at her cabin. Robert Long Foreman who lives with someone else's laundry, trying to understand why it was left to him. Michelle Pilar Hamill reading the texts, the people, and all that is unspoken in her young world, trying to figure a sense out of it.

At its best, the writing we share in these pages hands us some of what I seek among my father's papers: some sense to be made of a moment or an event that undoes us, some sense to be made when there is no one else to tell the story. Tracings. Taking up the matter of our lives—material, spiritual, genetic, malleable or rock-hard, inherited or invented, welcomed or not— and making something of it. This: what were you thinking?

We are often asking this question as we sit—separately or together—in the *Fourth Genre* office reading submissions. It's the question that often frames our editorial staff meetings each Friday when we bring pieces for a more extended discussion and consideration. This, I think, is why I'm a reader, and a writer, and an editor working to bring into print nonfiction essays. Thank you for sending them to us.

— *Laura Julier*

How to Run a Supermarket

PATRICIA PARK

START CONSTRUCTION

Begin with a plot of land in Brooklyn. An old building that once housed someone else's supermarket, someone else's *failed* supermarket. Your father picks it up for cheap at market and is banking on recouping that sweet shaded spot of profit under the efficiency curve. You wonder if your father has doubts—*Please Lord God don't let me fail like that other guy*—but that would only make him too human. He is a certain kind of person, the kind that does not believe in fear and trembling. Your mother is the opposite kind of person. You keep telling yourself you are the perfect blend of both. As you grow up, it will become increasingly apparent that you are more like your mother.

The store requires a gut renovation. A rewiring of the entire electrical nervous system. Ditto the plumbing. Before the supermarket was someone else's failed supermarket, it used to be a Catholic church. This presents an architectural quandary: do you bust open the second floor to expose the cathedral ceiling? Or rebuild the second floor and double the square footage, double the merchandise? But a supermarket with super-high ceilings presents a ConEd bill nightmare, and no one has ever heard of a two-story supermarket, at least not in those days. Better to keep it all at ground-level, with a new drop ceiling. This means there are only 50 square feet to devote to the office, where your mother will sit on a milk crate and count the day's totals, neck craned over the low wall to watch for shoplifters and shoplifting cashiers alike.

You and your older brother are the only ones in your elementary school familiar with the term "building code." (Your older sister is *not* the only one in her high school familiar with it.) Unlike you, your sister and brother actually

2 ◣ FOURTH GENRE

understand what it means, along with all the other terms your father brings home from the store: "building permits," "inspectors," "water bills," "liens." But you know they are the reason why suddenly the back of your father's station wagon looks like a tool shed, and there are scary dentist's office masks, and everything is covered with a thin film of dust and pulverized mouse droppings.

Mouse droppings. Mice, mice everywhere, but you can never *see* them. Your father learns to think like a mouse. Dinner discussions are so consumed with mice you might as well be eating them. Napkins are scribbled with dotted zigzags, representing a mouse's flight path. Cereal boxes are diagrammed in blueprints for traps. At that young age, you wish you could understand mechanics, acceleration, and trajectory, to contribute something meaningful to the conversation. Your mother, who has nothing useful to contribute, busies herself with clearing the dishes. You think of telling your father about a commercial you saw for a board game called Mouse Trap, and maybe the whole family can play together and learn to think like mice. But then you would be admitting you were watching the TV when he wasn't around (when the cat's away, so to speak), and besides, your father doesn't like interruptions. You made that mistake once before, when you told him you wrote a story about a messy schoolgirl, complete with stick figure illustrations. But you stopped when his eyes flashed a funny red.

At Sunday school you tell the whole class your father is a policeman. You fool no one; everyone in that room (your teacher included) is the son or daughter of deli-groceries, of dry cleaners, of nail salons.

Once construction is complete, the supermarket looks like two disparate eras—the Industrial, the Gothic—spliced together. The ground-level has an encased steel foyer with automated doors and windows covered in large posters advertising the week's sales. The building abruptly gives way to a soaring cathedral roof, along with a round, gaping space where once a stained glass pane reflected the westbound sun.

Learn Your Demographic

Later, the realtors will coin a catchy alliteration for this part of the borough: "Brownstone Brooklyn." But for now it's mostly middle class, mostly Italians, with the occasional overflow from the projects. (Perhaps only occasional because *Cosa Nostra* keeps that overflow at bay.) The customers' accents are so thick you could whir a deli slicer through them. You don't much care for the outer-borough twang, having learned your English from your older siblings, who learned their English from the television.

They film the very Italian movie *Moonstruck* in the very Italian bakery down the block from your supermarket, the same bakery where you swap your tens and twenties for their quarters, singles, and fives.

Because the neighborhood is mostly Italian, you carry Italian-American merchandise. You still have Middle-American grocery items like loaves of Wonder Bread, Kraft "cheese product" in individual plastic sleeves, jars of Hellmann's mayonnaise. But in the produce section there are heads of radicchio for trecolore salad, arugula bunches, and both kinds of parsley: the kind they use to garnish plates at fancy restaurants on TV, and the flat kind that gets stuck in your teeth after you bite into one of the deli-man's meatballs. The deli-man your father hires fills the display cases with *antipasto* of roasted red peppers and zucchini, tortellini salads dressed in red wine vinaigrette, and tomato-basil-cucumber salads. Over a bucket of murky water he kneads balls of mozzarella into cohesion. (Then he dumps the murky water down the drain, clogs the plumbing, and gets into a fight with your father.) Something is always sizzling or bubbling on the stove: minced garlic, breaded discs of eggplant, marinara sauce in a blackened pot. Hanging above the display case is a curtain of air-cured sausages dangling from strings, and below are decorative boxes of imported panettone (you don't much care for panettone; despite the powdered sugar on top, it tastes dry and spicy like licorice sticks).

Your father hires an Italian butcher, who stocks the refrigerated cases with the normal cuts of cow (sirloin, T-bone), and the not-so-normal: tripe, which looks like an old white sponge, and tongue, and heart. The butcher also makes pinwheels—skewered rolls of veal stuffed with flat-leaf parsley, parmesan cheese, and prosciutto—which a customer can toss into her basket after work and throw straight into the frying pan. This is an example of what you call value-added merchandise.

On weekends and school breaks you are enlisted as a bag packer. You quickly learn that the worst thing you can do is make a customer feel as though she has been cheated. This happens when you are stingy with the bags. Customers like lots of bags. Paper or plastic or paper and plastic. Bread in a separate bag. Eggs in a separate bag. Entenmann's cakes—windowpanes face-up—in a separate bag. One time a customer demands each of her items be packed in its own bag. McCormick's salt shaker. McCormick's pepper shaker. GE 60-watt light bulb. At the end of the transaction she collects her bags and beams, the way you might when you pull into a parking spot with a busted meter.

Your family is met with a mixed reception; not too many of your kind round these parts. But the neighborhood has long been awaiting a supermarket, so you are tolerated. You best not disappoint; when you do, you will hear about it. Once, a woman shouts to your mother, "Fuck you people! I'm never shopping here again." Your mother bows her head—*Sorry, I'm so sorry*, she mumbles—as the woman marches out the automated door. It is one of the first times you hear the F-word, but you intuit its meaning. Based on your mother's reaction, you're not sure she does. You get mad at her for not getting mad. *How come you let that woman talk to you like that?* Your mother is zen. *Lose one customer, lose one thousand customer.* One week later the customer is back, shopping cart brimming with merchandise.

It becomes something of a running mantra for you, a life equation: *lose one customer, lose one thousand customer.* Lose one thousand customer, you, your brother, and your sister will lose your college funds.

Learn to Multitask

It is busy and you jump from one cashier lane to the next, bagging groceries. "Paper or plastic?" you ask. You're thrown a curveball—"delivery"—which means you reach for a box. Apple boxes are most ideal, with their sturdy sides and matching lids; banana boxes are the worst and must be fitted with a square of cardboard to cover the gaping hole at the bottom. There are no apple boxes left, so you are forced to make do with a banana box. The customer's items come down the conveyor belt like a Tetris game, and you've already mapped out their configurations in the box. Heavy items—two-liters of Coca-Cola, a jug of Mott's Apple Juice—to the outsides, to evenly distribute the weight. Dannon Fruit on the Bottom Yogurt containers stacked one on top of the other so nothing will puncture their foil and plastic-lidded covers. Barilla spaghetti boxes upright and fitted into the corners, but if their tops spill over the lip they'll get crushed. You invent little games like this to get through the day: a job perk, if you will. You are only eight items in, when the customer begins arguing with the cashier because an item scanned at regular price. "That's on sale, five for four!" she insists. The cashier gives her a tired look; you abandon your packing to check the price. You speed down the aisle to the dairy section, spotting a toppled pyramid of Carnation Condensed Milk cans (mental note: fix display). When you reach the refrigerated open cases lining the back of the store, the sign below the Dannon Fruit on the Bottom yogurt containers says, "Yoplait Yogert 5/$4" (mental note: fix typo). As you rush back to the cash register to inform the customer, a new customer grabs you: "Where's Rose's Lime Juice?" You are too young for mixed drinks and don't recognize the product, so you point her down the produce aisle instead of the beverage aisle (mental note: learn new product). You've got to get back to that first customer. Again you pass the still-toppled Carnation displays on your way back (mental note: send one of the idle delivery boys to fix). You crane your neck—now there are torn Snickers Fun-Size bar wrappers tucked behind the cans. Doubling back to snatch the wrappers (mental note: has someone been eating on the job?), you collide with the White Rose delivery guy wielding a handtruck, who hands you an invoice for eight cases of . . . you cannot read the faded purple ink of the invoice. You say, "Let's walk and talk." Snickers Fun-Size wrappers are crumpled in your hand, and back at the register, you try—discreetly—to deposit them in the trash bin under the register (you fool no one: now the customer and cashier alike think *you're* the one eating on the job), then inform the customer (politely) that the Yoplait, not the Dannon Fruit on the Bottom, is the yogurt on sale. She whips a circular from her pocketbook: a big red circle marks the spot where the Dannon Fruit on the Bottom 6oz containers are listed, on sale, 5/$4. But she's holding last week's circular, not this week's (mental note: dispose of last week's circular). You wrestle with the quickest—and most diplomatic—way to phrase this to the customer, when suddenly there's a big, exasperated exhalation behind you and it's coming from the delivery guy; you are *this close* to telling him you are *his* customer, but you're only in junior high and he looks like he could beat the shit out of you with one hand behind his back, if he wanted. Meanwhile the woman with the circular's got her hands on her hips and homicide in her eyes, wielding back to throw you a verbal one-two combo. Suddenly you remember the mantra *the customer is always right*; you use that side of your brain that forces your face into a smile, you void out the transaction, and instruct the cashier to honor last week's sale price. The cashier snaps: this better not mess up my register totals. You stare down at the banana box of groceries. While you were away confirming the price of the item you now end up voiding and giving to the customer for the sale price anyway just to buy her silence so she won't bad-mouth the store, the cashier had finished packing the customer's items, and it is clear she has never played a game of Tetris in her life. Hers is a haphazard packing job guided by only the vaguest sense of geometry and ergonomics. The top-halves of spaghetti boxes flail out of the box, ready to be snapped in half when they hit the delivery boy's handtruck. A mushy package of Sargento's Shredded Pepper Jack lies at the bottom, bearing the weight of Jello-O Pudding Snacks six-packs, Nabisco Graham Crackers, and Honey-Nut Cheerios. Two liters of Coke and Mott's are stacked asymmetrically to one end of the box, causing the lifter to double-over to one side. But it's too late to repack the box. Then the phone rings; you answer—a customer cries, "I bowaht hayam from da deli theyuh layast week and now it's spoyuld!"—and the delivery guy lets out another deliberate sigh (mental note: tell your father to log in a complaint with the vendor; where *is* your father? You remember: inside the meat department's freezer walk-in box with a Phillip's head, a can of WD-40, and a manual; mental note: check on your father). As you attempt to calm down the customer on the phone, the Rose's Lime Juice customer has found you and demands you show her where exactly this elusive product is on the shelf. The mental notes pile up like stray coupons or bottle deposit slips that will never get cashed in.

All of seven minutes have gone by. In that seven minutes you have not completed a single task from start to finish, not even that Tetris game. You cannot imagine the reality of your parents' every day: 111 times a day, 364 days a year (you're closed Christmas Day). When classmates ask what you did over the school break, you say, not much. Not much at all.

Get to Know Your Employees

There are those who stay and those who come and go through the automated steel doors. The ones who leave leave for love, money, travel, deportation, fraud. The ones who stay stay for family, always family.

There was the Filipino Communist cashier, who gave away groceries for free, a racket that lasted a year longer than it should have. There was the Arab deli boy who abruptly quit, saying he felt "uncomfortable" in the workplace. But you can read between the lines: you've seen the sideways glances the Italian deli-man would cast his way. This was the same Italian deli-man who missed a week of work with no word and still your father could not fire him; he was Union. There was the Iranian cashier who fell in love with the Mexican stock boy—a man almost double her age and half her size—and divorced him months later. There was the Korean manager who struck the Korean assistant manager and, when fired, cut the credit card wires and emptied the contents of the safe. And before all that there was the Korean manager who worked loyally for your father for ten years, quit to move his family down to Florida to open his own business, failed, and moved his family back up to New York, and begged for his job back.

Then there are the Moroccan stock boys who open their wallets to show you pictures of their little girls: grinning, toothless toddlers who go on to work for the mayor's office. There is the Chinese cashier who worked side-by-side with her daughter to help her pay for med school. There's the half-Italian, half-Arab cashier who invites your whole family to her wedding. There's the Italian butcher whose wife sends handmade, seven-layer rainbow cookies every Christmas, and every Christmas it becomes your tradition, too, to cram as many of them into your mouth before your mother snatches the tray and hides it under an overturned kimchi pot. When the butcher retires, your father laments the lack of good butchers in a dying industry, and you lament your Italian cookie hook-up.

BRING YOUR WORK HOME WITH YOU

The kitchen counter is covered with bills, bills, this month's *Progressive Grocer,* more bills, a newsletter from the supermarket association, and stray coupons. The shelves are filled with the refuse of the supermarket (a mere pit-stop before your mother reluctantly tosses them into the garbage can): torn packages of Rizzoli farfalle, dented cans of (you hope) tuna fish with the labels filched off, ripped bags of Goya green lentils (since when does your family eat lentils? Or bowtie pasta, for that matter?). The refrigerator crisper is a cornucopia of bruised peaches, bruised tomatoes, bruised pomegranates, and wilted red-leaf lettuce.

You seldom cross paths with your father; usually he gets home just as you're about to go to bed. On rare nights when the family is assembled together, he conducts strategy huddles; you become a family of supermarket conspirators. Spread before him are more endless diagrams, no longer of mousetraps. Aisle layout designs and floor plans are scribbled on the backs of napkins, tissue boxes, the thin margins of newspapers. He talks of burgeoning food trends—something called "organics." He talks of profit margins, net and gross.

BARRON'S, FORBES, WALL STREET JOURNAL, THE SUNDAY NEW YORK TIMES

Your father lays flat clippings from these papers on the table. The articles' narratives are always the same: some young tyke takes over his parents' mom-'n-pop and ups its sales by a bajillion. Once, in a shopping frenzy, your father comes home with three copies of *How to Win Friends and Influence People,* one for each of you (none for your mother). This coming from the man who once took the family out to breakfast and refused to buy each of you your own bagel with cream cheese.

One time your father snaps open the paper to the stock section. "Abba gonna teach you how to reading stock quote," he announces. Your older sister gets it—she becomes an orthodontist. Your older brother gets it—he becomes an accountant. Only *you* don't get it. Your eyes wander to his hands: tanned, taut, and veiny, smeared with what you first take for newsprint ink, but then realize is machine grease. Your ears fixate on your father's dropped articles, his misconjugated verbs. Then your mind alights on your college application essay. You think about writing about your own writing. How it all began with *Messy Bessy,* your first illustrated (albeit unfinished, unpublished) manuscript penned in the first grade. You stop to ask your father if he thinks it's a good id—but Abba hate hate *hating the interruptions!* Red hairline veins crack over the whites of his eyes.

You remain quiet for the rest of the evening. But now your mind wanders to the tenor of your father's voice, and how if you had to assign it a color, it would be scalding red. A color that would match those eyes.

Learn to Cashier

In truth, you're a horrible cashier. You've managed this far to mask your deficiencies by excelling in bag-packing or price-checking or coupon-counting. Cashiering demands the performance of simultaneous hand-eye-brain functions: punching the keypad while staring at the merchandise in question while looking over at the screen to confirm that the right price appears and there are no system glitches while turning to pack the merchandise (if there are no delivery boys around to help) in paper or plastic or paper and plastic or boxes while maintaining good registerside manner (no gum smacking, no telling the customer she's wrong even when she's wrong). You are not horrible at any of these functions in isolation, but the supermarket is the antithesis of functions in isolation.

On the spot you mistake kale for collard greens, cilantro for parsley (a rookie mistake). In your haste to get through the stream of customers, your right pinky slips and you strike a zero instead of a nine. It slips again and strikes the "Produce" button instead of "Enter," ringing up a customer's red globe (seedless) grapes for $40.23. Cashiering is an endless game of Memory: matching produce items with their corresponding four-digit codes (PLUs, in industry parlance), then matching them back to their weekly (sometimes daily) fluctuating prices, by the count or by the pound. Cashiering requires extemporaneous arithmetic. An example: a customer's total comes to $11.38; she hands you a twenty and you punch 2-0-0-0 (the system auto-corrects for double-digits). The computer screen may tell you the difference is $8.62, but when she fishes in her bag for two singles, a dime, and three pennies, you must compute the new total—no pencils, no scientific calculators—to a nice even ten and three quarters (to feed the meter or the laundry jar). You must remember to give back the customer clean, crisp new bills, stacking the worn and torn singles, fives, and tens at the bottom of the register. You are convinced there is an untapped market for pairing high school students studying for the SATs with cashier jobs.

So why start cashiering now?

Because you got your college degree but no one will hire you. (Perhaps that's no surprise; after all, you did graduate from a college that accepted you based on an essay about an unkempt schoolgirl turned mother of 20—yes, you did end up writing about *Messy Bessy*—or so it said in the dean of admissions' hand-scribbled acceptance note.) College has taught you many things, like how to deconstruct your cashiering ineptitude through a number of multivariate theorems:

(1) Spotlight effect (all eyes are on you)
(2) Stereotype threat (you're a girl, and girls are supposed to be no good at math)
(3) Reverse stereotype threat (but you're Asian; aren't Asians supposed to be good at math?)
(4) Freudian neurosis (you're experiencing sensory overload; cf. Proust, *Remembrance of Things Past,* vol. I "Swann's Way")
(5) Piagetian critical period (you should've learned to cashier before you turned 12)
(6) Cognitive dissonance (you've spent the last four years deconstructing constructs like the aforementioned, and now you're faced with a task that employs a skillset that is in direct conflict with your newly-acquired skillset)

You know how to phrase your dilemma in the form of a Hegelian dialectic. What you don't know is how to scan items and pack them at the same time, the supermarket equivalent of chewing gum while walking down the street. The items' scan codes (UPC codes or SKU numbers, in industry-speak) have always looked to you like wrought-iron bars.

If you were a different kind of person, a person more like your father, you might have marched down to the local library for a copy of a *Complete Idiot's Guide to.* If you were a person more like your mother, you might have kept your head down until, with time, you honed your skills. But four years of college have taught you better than that: instead, you stage a rebellion. Little things at first: you speak in complete sentences ("If you could just bear with me for a moment, I will gladly process your refund") instead of two-word answers ("Yes, ma'am"). You eavesdrop on customer conversations and toss in your $0.02. Ten-cent words stud your speech. If your rebellion had a catchphrase, it would be: *There's more to this cashier than you think!* (If your rebellion had a subconscious Freudian agenda, you suspect it might be about your mother. As in: *Don't you dare talk to me like you talk to my mother. Just because a person drops her auxiliary verbs does not mean she is deaf and dumb.*)

One day, you hatch your master plan: to wear your college T-shirt to work. In retrospect it was stupid, but you get caught up in a fit of scheming. After a few hours, a customer finally comments on your shirt. "I thought you guys were way up here!" He holds his hand level with the crown of his silvery head. "Things must have gone downhill since." This was not the reaction you were hoping to elicit. Perhaps he sees the flush of embarrassment spreading over your cheeks because he quickly adds, "But hey, whatever pays the bills, right?" He hastens away. For the rest of the day, you wear a moth hole-ridden brown sweater you find in the back corner of the office, behind the milk crates. One week later, when a customer comes in wearing your same college T-shirt, you almost—*almost*—claim alumniship. Instead you look down and pack his salmon, his bundle of dill, his Vitamin Water. Your short-lived rebellion has been squelched.

You comfort yourself by thinking how none of your fellow classmates would last an hour in the store. In the same time it'd take you to ring up five customers' groceries at 20 items apiece (even though you're slower than all the other cashiers), they'd sit pensively, Sharpie in hand, pondering the wording of a Poland Spring water sales sign like they were coining a villanelle.

RELEARN YOUR DEMOGRAPHIC

The neighborhood is changing. The new arrivals are white, but not the olive-white of the neighborhood—theirs is pinkish-purple under a translucent film of skin. Their eyes are varying shades of Mayflower blue. They look like people from your college catalog. Gone are the old laundromat, the aforementioned Italian bakery, the old drugstore, the old social club. In their place: a holistic healing center, a café with free Wi-Fi, a drugstore-themed ice cream joint, a social club-themed cocktail bar. "The Italians, they don't like change," one of your Italian cashiers, born and bred in the 'hood, tells you. It sounds like an omen. Still, the change must go on.

And with it an overhaul in merchandise. The refrigerator cases are filled with new merchandise: organic cottage cheese and Greek yogurt, along with tubs of something called baba ghanoush. Those dry, bland German crackers you used to find while rummaging the cupboards for snacks in the eighties are now back on the shelves. Everything is organic; then everything is green; then everything is gluten-free.

The new customers bring their own bags. This is a new concept to you: pack your bags using *your* bags? These bags, made of vinyl or cloth, say things like Whole Foods, Fairway, Trader Joe's. But to err is human: sometimes these customers forget to BYOB. When that happens, they exhale air in exaggerated huffs to stop you from loading their groceries into a second bag. You're still not sure whether this is better than having customers think you're stiffing them.

Sometimes "second-generationers" come into the store. They always look like they are coming from *real* work: suit, briefcase, shiny shoes. When you transact, they do not look you in the eye. You wonder if you remind them of their own parents, of their own neglected filial duties. Before your father bought this store, he used to own the supermarket on Smith. New owners now run that store. You go in once, to check it out. You want to buy one can from a six-pack. The second-generation son demands you buy the entire six-pack. But you know better; you look him in the eye and inform him each can has its own UPC code. He makes you buy the entire six-pack. (People sometimes confuse their store with yours. But your store smells of recycled refrigerated air, spicy arugula, and cold cuts. Their store smells of fish.)

Your store's new customers are not like the Italians. The Italians put up a fight but they always pay in cash. The new customers speak in a honeyed *sotto voce* as they hand over their cards. Debit or credit? you ask. Credit, they say. Always credit.

Expect Changes in Your Personal Life

Over time, the store will change you. First, you wear sneakers everywhere and take to massaging your calf muscles even in public. Then your speech: it's clipped. You trim away the wordy excess and begin to enjamb words. Your eyes, ears, nose, and throat grow keen to inefficiencies, and you soon realize *everything* is inefficient. The line at the DMV. The way your friends spread in a zigzag on the sidewalk outside a restaurant. Why are you the only one standing with your back against the wall, making way for passing handtrucks? After dinner you stop in a corner store and each of your friends files out with a 20 ounce bottle of Diet Coke, retailing almost two dollars a pop; it dawns on not one of them that they could have each chipped in 40 cents for a two-liter instead.

The concept of a weekend seems like a luxury, an indulgence. When friends complain of 40-, 60-, 80-hour work weeks spent sitting in a chair, you think of miniature violin symphonies. They suggest drinks at that new social club-themed cocktail bar a few blocks from your father's store. You remember when it was still an operating social club. You order a beer and compute its 400 percent markup. You are all there to cruise, but when you see customers from the store you avert your eyes to the ground.

Your boyfriend of a brief duration—an aspiring academic—moves into a new apartment; you are enlisted to help. He, his brother (a lawyer), and his brother's girlfriend (one of those PR girls) stand and gape at the gaping-open U-Haul. "Let's pause for a moment to think about how we should plan to do this," your boyfriend says. But what's there to think about? You've played this Tetris game before and the rental van return time's a-tickin.' But like your mother you keep your trap shut. Ten minutes later they are still thinking while you have made your third trip up and down the three-flight brownstone. The boxes are heavy in your arms, like the delivery for a customer hosting an Independence Day party (two-liters of soda, glass jars of salsa and dip, and one too many gallon jugs of water). You feel like one giant yellow workhorse. The PR girlfriend of the brother, now wife (you know this because you will see the ring when she hands you her credit card years later at the store), has the good sense to lean against the van to make way for you, and your boyfriend's boxes.

You are convinced the world is divided into two kinds of people: those who have common sense, and those who do not. Sometimes it feels like everyone from the latter camp talks in slo-mo. You feel the red blood pulsing behind your eyes as you listen to them speak: so slowly, so painfully slowly, do their words emerge.

◥ ◥ ◥

You've always known you weren't wired for this job. Because no matter how long you've been doing it, there will always be a hitch in your flustered movements. The way your fingers stall at the trigger of a price gun because you cannot remember the Suggested Retail Price of the steel cut oat canisters staring back at you, waiting to be stickered. The same Suggested Retail Price you had attempted to calculate off the invoice of the distributor three times until you finally had to call for your father, who computed the formula in his head—no pencils, no scientific calculators—and rattled off the prices quicker than you could jot them down. There will always be something too forced, too obsequious, about the way you smile at customers, desperate not to lose their business. At night you lie twitching awake, replaying each and every one of their multivariate complaints: *Why are your plastic bags so thin? Why aren't your plastic bags environmentally friendly? Why doesn't anyone here speak English?*, along with your corresponding bumbling responses: *I'm sorry.* Always, *I'm sorry.*

Your father makes a proposal: he wants you to take over the store. He wants for you a better life, better than the life of sitting behind a computer never knowing when you're going to get fired, better than the life he left behind when he boarded the ship to the Americas.

You make a list of everything you know about how to run a supermarket. Then a list of all the things you don't know. What you realize is this: that second list is long, much longer than the first.

The Third Step

SHERYL ST. GERMAIN

Made a decision to turn our will and our lives over to the care of God as we understood Him.

—The Big Book of Alcoholics Anonymous

My friend's son was killed last week. A young soldier, having fought in Afghanistan, he had come home for a time and was waiting to be deployed again in a few days. He was a man who loved the army, so his mother and the obituaries would say. He took his motorcycle out last Tuesday to visit the wife and child of a friend and fellow soldier still in Afghanistan. Perhaps it was a sunny day like this one, a blue sky, a spring day when trees are budding and the first fragile flowers are blooming close to the ground. Perhaps it felt like a day of hope, a day he intended to comfort his friend's wife, to assure that her husband would return.

He was a good man like that, so his mother said, so the obituaries said, a man kind to children, though he had none. He had been traveling on his motorbike, obeying the speed limit, his mother says, on some highway in Arkansas, when someone in a truck made a bad decision, pulled out in front of him, and that was it. Not even the full-face helmet he was wearing could save him.

I don't much like churches, but I have come to this one, a Catholic church in the hills of Pittsburgh, for my friend, to attend the funeral mass of her son. The truth is I don't mind churches of almost any faith but Catholic, because non-Catholic churches are a mystery to me, and I sort of like the mystery of unfamiliar churches and religions. They demand nothing of me, they remind me of nothing, they are often pleasant in the way that visiting a new park is pleasant. You look around at the people hanging out, at the playground equipment, the flowerbeds and trees, you walk around a bit, smile at the kid on a skateboard or a dog sniffing a bush, and then you go home. You have not been changed, nothing has been asked of you, no bad memories have been brought to light.

But I was raised Catholic, forced to attend Catholic school for nine years before I turned away from it for what still feels like forever. I know way too much about the Catholic Church to be able to relax in one as I might in, say, a Protestant church or a mosque or synagogue. I am nervous, on guard, constantly waiting for something to go wrong. I know too much about the failings of the weak men who have sometimes sat as popes and the equally weak men who have served as priests and preyed on young boys, too much about the failings of the Church dogma, especially in matters concerning women, too much about the witch trials of centuries past. I have been personally wounded by its failing to provide a meaningful spiritual compass for me as a child and young adult. Its rote questions and answers. Its stiff rites and sacraments. *Where do the souls of the brain-dead go*, I asked a priest many years ago as my young brother lay in a coma from a drug overdose. He couldn't tell me.

I haven't been to a Mass in many years and I haven't taken Communion in maybe 25 years. While I do believe a man like Jesus may have lived a life not unlike the one that comes down to us in the New Testament, there's not a bone in my body I can force to believe in a god that allows such treachery and quackery to go on in his name.

Although of course every bone in my body wants to believe.

Sitting here in this church, near the front, hoping my friend can see that I'm here to support her, looking at all the trappings of that religion I have come to so distrust—the priests in their special funeral garb, the cross of the nailed Christ in the center, as horrifying as I remember from childhood, the statues of Mary and minor saints in the apses, all the candles lit, the altar with its Book of Gospels, the incense, the pews and the kneelers—I have wildly varying sensations: of disgust that rises like bile in my throat so thick I feel in any moment I will throw up, of great sadness for my friend, for her family, especially her daughter who cannot stop sobbing, for the army men and women sharing this pew all stiff and mournful in their dress uniforms, men and women who were my friend's son's colleagues and friends. I cannot stop crying myself, although I did not know the dead man. Sitting in the hard pew I feel myself literally present but also thrust back, sitting in a similar pew for the death of my brother seven years ago, and forward, sitting here for my beautiful son, who is this dead son's age and who has been drinking himself into oblivion for many years now. Who will attend his funeral? Will I sit here alone, with no family, no god, no faith? I am reminded of how my alcoholic father had alienated so many at the end that only a few family members came to his funeral.

I don't tend to like soldiers as a rule, but I like these, standing all tall and smart, wearing their medals and badges of honor, as my father, also a soldier, used to do at special occasions. My heart grieves for them, and for the rag-tag motorcycle group also here, with their long hair and polished motorcycles, standing brave and proud in chains and leather outside of the church, they too honoring one of their own.

The coffin is in the center aisle, draped with an American flag. I watch as the soldiers take the flag off and fold it carefully into a triangle to give to the dead one's mother, and listen as the priest says his words over the body of this soldier he did not know, and I wonder if these ceremonies can matter to anyone at all except for those present.

I do not feel this space as a sacred space except for the fact that it contains a group of people who feel sacred to me, a community of women and men on a path to sobriety. My friend is one of these, and sprinkled among the mourners from the blood family, the army family, and the motorcycle family are we, members of that community.

I too am trying to live a life of sobriety. I am trying not to fall into the death that my father and brother fell into, the one I fear my son also seems to be facing. Twice he has called me in the last year to tell me he felt he would die if he didn't stop drinking, that he felt a death rattle, and more than once he has tried to stop but failed. I can only listen and take it in, I can only stop myself; I can't stop him.

I am working on the third step, trying to give my life over to the care and will of a higher power, struggling to believe in a higher power that is not this god on the crucifix. I stare at the nails hammered into Jesus's hands and feet and wonder what it would feel like to hang from a cross.

We shouldn't mourn that my friend's son died like this, in an accident, the priest is saying, we shouldn't mourn that he didn't die an *honorable* death in a war; any death, he says, is an honorable death if the life one lived was honorable. I look at the ribs in Christ's torso, the crown of thorns, the look of resignation on his face. How can I give the care and will of my life up to this?

I've explored goddess religions, animism, even Voodoo and Condemblé. I have explored every kind of spiritualism that seemed to offer possibility of a belief in something larger than me, but either they have failed me or I have failed them, I cannot say which. This god hanging on the cross, the god that shaped my formative years, is only a reminder of how far I have come and how much I have failed to find what my new family calls a higher power.

When my friend finally walks up to the pulpit and has a chance to speak of her son, I look at her face and try to force Christ out of my mind, although it's impossible to look to the front of the church and not see the Christ hanging on the cross. I force his image to recede into the background and focus on my friend. She speaks of her son's life, telling some funny stories. She's strong and gentle and fair to everyone who is grieving, even her ex-husband, who sits crumpled in the front pew. She's a spiritual powerhouse, many years sober, and I want to be like her; I want her to be my higher power. I want to be able someday to stand in a church, like her. I don't want to be this trembling mess of fear that I sometimes am.

When I call my sponsor later to talk about the funeral she reminds me that she and my friend have worked the steps many times for many years, for both themselves and those they sponsor, that it has taken work for them to get where they are, that I should stop beating myself up about it. I'm still young, two years old in that world, and stumbling my way through the steps.

She, my sponsor, took me to a monastery a few weeks ago to talk me through the third step. I told her I am willing to turn my life over to a higher power but the truth is that I am willing but unable. I still feel stuck somehow, don't know what it means to have a caretaker that is not the God of the Old or New Testament.

Another of our tribe is here in the church singing. She has long dusty dreadlocks and is six months sober. She sings in a breathy voice, heavy as honey, that reminds me a little of Sarah McLachlan, "Then sings my soul, My Savior God, to Thee, How great Thou art! How great Thou art!" she sings, "Then sings my soul, My Savior God, to Thee, How great Thou art! How great

Thou art!" Over and over she sings the refrain, for what seems like a long time; there are stanzas that reference the beauty of the physical world as proof of God's greatness, the trees, the forests, the woods, the stars, the mountains. There is a stanza that focuses on the gift of God's son to us that leads once again to the refrain, "How great Thou art! How great Thou art!" and it hurts my soul to hear these words: can my singer friend really believe them, can my mourning friend, mother of the dead boy, really believe them? How can we be singing, on the day of such a death, *how great thou art*?

My friend is finished speaking, and the time for Communion has come. This is the moment in the Catholic Mass where one receives bread from the priest that is supposed to represent the body of Christ. It was always confusing to me, as a child, Communion. Was the bread a symbol or were we to believe it really was the body of Christ? It looked like a round, thin wafer, and none of the priest's chanting and incantations could change that. A wafer, not the body of God.

When I was younger we couldn't eat anything for three hours before Mass if we planned to have Communion, and we could not have Communion if we had any sins we had not confessed. The idea is that your body be clean both physically and spiritually, that you are literally preparing to ingest the body of God.

Now everyone is lining up for Communion, and it crosses my mind that perhaps I should consider taking it. A wave of revulsion rushes through me—I don't want to commune with or have anything to do with this religion. But I've said I'm giving my life to the care of a higher power, and wouldn't receiving Communion be a physical sign of that? My heart starts beating faster, and I can feel my knees trembling. Why am I here, I ask myself. What led me to enter this godforsaken church anyway? I look at the coffin, at my friend. I calm down. I see that my friend has taken Communion and is returning to her seat in the front pew. If I walk up to receive Communion I'll have to pass right by her. She'll see me. She'll know I'm here for her. I don't think she's seen me yet, since she arrived with her family and the coffin, and I've been hidden in the bowels of the church with all the other visitors. Maybe, I think, I should do this for her. I start my way down the pew, knowing that once I start there's no way to turn back. I keep going, although I'm frantically making an inventory of sins I might have committed in the last 25 years, since my last confession. I remember the face my mother used to make when my father took Communion during his once-a-year Christmas Mass, and I'm grateful she's not here to judge.

"He shouldn't be taking Communion," she would say, reminding the children that it was a mortal sin to miss Mass as much as he did, not saying what she must have known by then, that he was sleeping with other women, committing adultery.

Still, who was she to know what was in his heart? Perhaps he became, for a moment, the altar boy he had been when he was younger, perhaps he felt for a moment the faith and hope he'd felt as a boy and wanted to do something to honor it. Perhaps he had a momentary hope that taking Communion would help him to change his life.

I am not unlike many others who want to have faith, who idolize those who have it, but who ourselves have little faith; we "refuse it even the smallest entry," as the poet David Whyte writes in his poem "Faith." As I wait in line to take Communion I wonder if a small act like this, or some other small act, the writing of a small essay such as this one, might open one to faith?

I don't feel anything when I take the Communion wafer from the priest and put it in my mouth. I catch my friend's eye and she acknowledges seeing me, but I don't all of a sudden feel communed with God or filled with the Spirit. Truth be told I feel a bit like a fraud. The wafer seems exactly as it did 25 years ago, tasteless and sticky, as I've written elsewhere, like a stamp you'd licked that had gotten stuck in your mouth.

Still, I'm not unhappy that I took the walk. I'm glad I tried. The priest reads us something from Matthew: "Whatsoever you do to the least of my people, that you do unto me." Trying to swallow the wafer as elegantly as possible, I think, not for the first time, that perhaps god is in us, in my friends sitting in this church, not out in some abstract heaven.

"Our father who art in heaven," the priest starts, and we all chime in, "hallowed be thy name." It is the prayer with which we end every meeting of my recovery group. We always stand in a circle and hold hands. I'm always happy saying this prayer with my group although I don't believe in this god the father. I do believe in the people whose hands I am holding, though. It's the most powerful moment of the meeting for me: I feel an incredible electricity in the room, a raw power in the hands I am holding. It's as if for that moment I'm tuned to some kind of god radio station that's directly linked into whatever higher power it is for which I'm searching. And maybe that's just what I need to practice, tuning myself to some station, some frequency that channels what I feel in the rooms of those meetings.

"In the name of the Father, the Son, and the Holy Spirit," the priest is saying. "Amen," everyone is saying. The coffin is being escorted out, men with bagpipes are playing "Amazing Grace," we are all sobbing. The family follows the coffin, my friend leaning on her daughter, and then we all fall in, the soldiers, the motorcyclists, and the drunks, some of whom can find god's station even in darkness, others of us still fumbling to get the right reception.

What I Won't Wear

KATE CARROLL DE GUTES

MAC or Bobbi Brown. Maybelline and Cover Girl are out, too. Although Estée Lauder and L'Oreal make excellent moisturizers and everyone needs well-hydrated skin. And sometimes, I'll wear a little Aveda brand lipstick just to freak out my girlfriend and because, in a strange way, it's almost gender bending.

Mini-, midi-, or maxi-skirts. A-line, drop-waisted, jumper, or sundresses. A shirtwaist, a sheath, or a shift. A cocktail dress or a ball gown. A Kitty Foyle or a St. John's Knit. A tunic. A crinoline. A bustle. That said, I don't mind wrapping a Sarong around my waist (and over my shorts) to visit Catholic cathedrals in Latin countries. It's sort of my butch version of a skort. Although, it's not exactly flattering.

A twinset, cap-sleeved T-shirts, or anything called a blouse. A chemise, a spaghetti-strap tank top, or a tube top. A smock or a turtleneck (because I'm not a painter and my neck's too short). A shirt with a Peter Pan collar. A choli or anything where my midriff hangs out.

Nylons, thigh-high or otherwise. Of course, Spanx are a miracle of modern technology that our forebears fought for—a twenty-first-century alternative to the merrywidow—and which I believe have their place in the well-dressed butch's wardrobe.

Court shoes or elevator shoes. Platforms, stilettos, or kitten heels. No to mules and pumps, too. No to Manolo Blahnik, Jimmy Choo, Charles Jourdan, Christian Louboutin, and Bruno Magli. Unless you're talking about his two-tone oxford or the big-buckled, chunky-heeled loafer. But you're not, are you? You mean his wedges and his spectator pumps, don't you? In which case, no means no.

What I Will Wear

KATE CARROLL DE GUTES

It's fraught for all sorts of reasons.

Because when I came out it was not politically correct to be butch or femme—buying into the dominant paradigm of gender expectations and all that. Because I have been socialized as a woman even as I have railed against Maybelline and MAC, and all those ridiculous outfits that require you to sit with your thighs demurely pressed together. Because—and it pains me most to admit this one—I care what you think. I want you to like me and not judge me simply because I favor patterned ties in a double Windsor knot.

It's easy to dress for everyday. There's no issue with slim-fit, colored chinos—especially if they have a button fly. Burnt umber, cobalt, sage green, fire-truck red, and aubergine all hang in my closet. A hard finish so the pants wear well is preferable, but brushed twill is all right, too. Everyone is wearing these now. Even Costco sells Gloria Vanderbilt colored jeans for women. And if I wear mine rolled at the hem like a J. Crew male model or a Kennedy summering at Hyannis Port, you likely won't even notice.

Special events are more, shall we say, challenging. Do I wear the black, summer-weight wool, pinstriped pants, custom-made for my five-foot-four frame? Blue or black twill pants, the de rigueur look of business casual? Plain front or pleated? I'm starting to cross that gender line—now you're going to notice.

Crew neck T-shirts, I favor these. Long sleeve is, more often than not, better than short. Somehow it's more formal and completes my favored high-brow/low-brow look of jeans, a T-shirt, and an expensive vest or blazer. Of course, I also like hip shirts cut from Italian cotton and made by Bugatchi Uomo, Duchamp, or Robert Graham. Something with subtle checks, reversed out cuffs and collars, and square buttons, something that when paired with my perpetually flushed Irish cheeks and soft face gives me a gender-bending look. I'm afraid you'll notice my transgression, but I also love to transgress. See, I told you it's *fraught.*

But now the tie, bow and otherwise. Patterned more often than not. This is the big one. A tie is like a big fucking billboard that says, "Ask me about my gender identification!" Here's the rationalization that I make each time I'm standing in the mirror, collar up, tying under, over, behind, and through: a patterned tie is ornamental, and loose at the neck, charming, with less chance of people thinking you're just an angry dyke trying to make a point. And please don't call me that unless you are. A dyke, I mean. Straight people— even liberal ones— don't get to use that word.

The shoes. Ropers and cowboy boots can work. Frye boots if it's a hipster event—same thing with biker-toe black oxfords. For meeting clients or dinners out, suede wingtips or saddle shoes with outrageously garish laces are stylish and whimsical. Wingtips made with shiny Cordovan leather dyed tobacco brown or midnight black are too much. Too much what, I'm not entirely sure. Too butch, yes. Too gender nonconforming when paired with the rest of my ensemble, sure. Too much of an in-your-face statement, maybe. Even though these shoes feel right on me, I don't think I have the ego-strength to carry off wearing them.

Finally, the foundation. Boxers or briefs? Sports or push-up bra? Wouldn't you like to know.

Third Ear

D A V I D   N A I M O N

don't remember the sounds at all—not the voice of our driver, not the call of the chai wallahs, not the rumbling traffic—when we first arrived in Varanasi. But I do remember the corpse. Lucie and I were riding in a taxi from the airport, through streets choked with rickshaws, motorbikes, turbaned men, veiled women, ownerless cows, and dogs that somehow slept in the road amid the mayhem. Their dreaming canine heads, surrendering to fate, lay perilously close to the traffic. Yet somehow they lived and slept on peacefully.

We had talked to several friends about their trips to India and when asked where we should go, they didn't hesitate. "Varanasi," they said. "The best and worst of India, its ugliness and its beauty in one place." We decided to start our journey there, not knowing at the time that it would be the only place we would see in India, and that our trip would be cut short.

The arrival, after 36 hours of transit from Oregon, was a hallucinatory experience. Orange-robed holy men with painted faces, scraggly beards, and walking sticks, hobbling right out of an ancient story, next to businessmen in Western suits, busily chatting on their cell phones or texting. Women hidden in shapeless black burqas jostled in the market with those whose bare bellies peeked out from colorful saris and scarves.

The corpse was right in front of us the whole time, but we didn't know it. Not until the driver pointed it out atop the ramshackle van ahead of us in traffic. Strings of orange flowers cascaded over the mound that rode atop the car. "An old man," the driver said. "You can tell by the color of his shroud." Down below the body, through the half-open back doors of the van, were the countless drawn faces of the family, the mourners, staring vacantly at us, or past us, stuffed into the back of the vehicle that barreled toward the Old City

◥ 27

along the Ganges. "People come from all around," the driver said. "Three to four hundred bodies are burned here each day. Some by an electrical method, most by fire."

Even staring us in the face, however, death remained abstract to us. It hid beneath those flowers, behind fascinating and unfamiliar ritual. The day we actually felt death's breath on our necks was still two days away.

We quickly fell in love with the city that refused to keep life and death separate, each one alternating and overlapping from moment to moment, place to place. The pedestrian labyrinth of alleyways could lead you to either one. A delightfully sunny path, the wafting smells of incense, chai, and fried dosas, a troop of monkeys sifting through some leaves, goats standing on a bench, supplicants waiting to enter a temple. Or down a dark and forsaken street, marked by excrement and trash, unbelievable stench, standing water, and shadow.

The river itself, arising from the purest of Himalayan sources, was polluted by industrial effluent, the corpses of cows, the bones of the cremated, the bodies of holy men and children weighted down and sunk by stones. Yet pilgrims bathed there as if the water had traveled untouched from its rocky spring source. And we felt like we had traveled untouched as well. We had heard from so many how difficult traveling in India was, but found everything to be easy and inviting. Things flowed, the way the swarm of human, animal, and vehicular traffic seemed to magically flow along without incident, wheels avoiding the heads of dogs as if an unseen hand orchestrated the whole thing.

Our last night in Varanasi was only our third of a planned six. We had just returned from a trip to the town of Sarnath, where the Buddha gave his first sermon. Temple murals there depict the Buddha's life—his birth, his spiritual battles, his enlightenment. But it was the Buddha's ears that particularly captivated me. Unusually long, hanging almost to his shoulders when in meditation pose, his ears seemed even larger in the deathbed scene. Here the Buddha lay on his side and appeared at first to have one hand under his head. But a closer look showed the hand to be in front of the ear that rested on his pillow, slightly cupped as if listening for something. I wondered what he was listening for. Some Buddhists say the large ears symbolize his compassion, his all-hearing of the suffering of others. I imagined he was hearing sounds from the other side of the life-death divide.

Varanasi, despite its proximity to this Buddhist pilgrimage site, is mainly Hindu, and its exalted place in Hinduism is the equivalent of Jerusalem or Mecca for Jews and Muslims. Die in Varanasi and receive *moksha*, liberation from the cycle of rebirth, release from the wheel of life and death. That night, we walked along the Ganges, from ghat to ghat, steep and long staircases that descend to the landings by the river, serving both as points of orientation and places to gather. We were headed to the nightly puja ceremony, a series of Hindu rituals performed outside a nearby temple shortly after dark. The night before, we had walked the other direction and had come, inadvertently, to the edge of the main "burning ghat," where the majority of the corpses are cremated on multiple large funeral pyres. A man identified himself as an untouchable, told us that all the people who tended to the corpses and their remains were from this lowest of castes, and offered to walk us through the area. Every nook and cranny of available space was stacked high with endless cords of wood. Even the boats that floated just beyond the landing had looming log towers on them that dwarfed the huddled boatmen below.

Several bodies were in various stages of burning, separated by caste. Smoke snaked through the ghat making our eyes water, forcing us to shift location according to the wind. Cows wandered through the scene, goats picked through the debris, dogs slept on the warm ash, often nestled startlingly close to the fire itself. Various men positioned and repositioned the shrouded bodies, tending and stoking the fires.

At one point several men came barreling down an alleyway carrying a very large forked stick whose end contained a smoking blackened thing that at first I thought was the charred entrails of an animal. Our guide informed us that once the bodies were burned, the purified bony remains of the chest of a man, or the pelvis of a woman, would be dropped into the river to finish the ceremony, much as these men were doing. He showed us the original fire, started by the god Shiva 5,000 years ago, from which each of these funeral pyres were lit. We learned that criminals and the poorest of the poor were burned nearby by a cheaper electrical method. And that the two haunted-looking windowless buildings that hovered over the pyres, coated in the soot and dust of countless years of cremation, were occupied by untouchables without family, who were sick or old and waiting to die, hoping, thanks to the good will of others, to raise enough money for the wood for their own eventual cremations.

But tonight we were headed in the other direction, toward the music, the color, the festivity, toward life. Thousands of people gathered at the puja ceremony each night, the majority Indians, but a significant minority of tourists like ourselves, to watch the elaborate ritual offerings to the gods. To get there you must pass through a gauntlet of "touts," hard-selling entrepreneurs for which Varanasi is notorious, who pester you at every move, offering everything from hashish to a boat ride to a palm reading to a guided tour. And nowhere in Varanasi is this more prevalent than along the river. Despite the warnings and grumblings in the guidebooks, they didn't bother us much at all. In fact, we had struck up a good rapport with many of them. Many, like Sunil the boatman and Radhu, who toured us through the crematorium, remembered our names and would wave and call out to us from across the ghats, a friendly greeting each time we ventured from our guesthouse.

That isn't to say that walking the Ganges in Varanasi didn't involve some strategizing. The day before, when a young man came up to me, grabbed my hand without invitation, wedged his thumbs into the flesh of my palm, and pushed the little bones of my hand apart with the strength of a wrestler, I realized even a friendly handshake could go awry. "Massage, just ten minutes," he said, already holding my shoulder and twisting the muscles of my forearm as if trying to pull it apart like chicken from the bone.

But tonight we made it to the puja ceremony without incident. The crowd seemed relaxed and captivated, clapping along as the various red-clad performers on the riverside platform invited the gods through a series of synchronized divine offerings of fruit and flowers, incense and fire.

After a while we made our way to a smaller puja ceremony at the next ghat and were stopped by a little girl, perhaps six years old, who offered to paint designs on Lucie's hands. "No thank you," we said. Undeterred, she opened a box of tiny glass bottles full of colored ointments, proceeded to quickly dip a small metallic instrument in a purple one, and then before we could move on, pressed it upon the back of Lucie's hand, creating a stylized circle. Lucie looked up, met my eyes, and smiled a helpless but happy smile.

The girl then dipped another instrument in a silver ointment and began to create a radial pattern, like a flower or a sun. But she was soon pushed aside by a taller girl. "She's my sister," the older one said as she continued the interrupted pattern on my wife's hand, a pattern she would never finish.

Later people told us it was the loudest sound they had ever heard. Lucie and I heard nothing at all. I remember feeling a wind against my legs, seeing debris flying at the periphery of my vision, the sensation as if my head had been plunged deep underwater, the sound of my screams trapped inside my head. And then, though I do not recall flying through the air, do not remember landing or standing up, I was standing again, and knew somehow that a moment before I was not. And that's when I saw her. The rest of the world became a blank screen, its sole purpose to highlight her presence before it. Lucie lay crumpled on the ground, face-down amid a pile of cement debris, curled up as if asleep. And she wasn't moving.

I remember my movements then as slow, dream-like, and silent. Yet everything that happened was instantaneous. I yelled her name. I pulled her up. We ran, our hands over our ears.

We ran past the first puja ceremony, whose performers were still calmly doing their synchronized rites even though the crowd had dispersed. How was this possible? Why weren't they fleeing? Perhaps a speaker blew or it was a fireworks mishap, I thought. As we ran from ghat to ghat toward our guesthouse we passed people running *toward* the sound, toward us, and past us, from all parts of town. "What happened? What happened?" they asked. We shook our heads. We didn't know. "A bomb for sure," they replied.

The guesthouse was locked down, a big iron gate pulled across its shuttered entrance. We were led through a side door. Panicked family members and friends rushed to see if we were their loved ones returning from the river. Others trickled in. Several travelers left immediately for the airport or train station, pulling on their large rucksacks and braving the dark labyrinth of alleyways to get to the main road. Others argued that airports and train stations had been targets in the past and were no safer than here—in fact, far less so. Several people held their ears like we did.

Still not fully believing what was happening, I refreshed the news feed on the computer in the lobby over and over again. A two-year old Indian girl dead. Other bombs found that had not detonated. An Italian in critical condition. "It's not my fault," yelled the guesthouse owner. "It's not my fault," he repeated, as an irate guest who had just arrived that day left without paying.

Within hours, photos appeared on the screen. An exploded staircase, an obliterated blue railing twisted beyond recognition. The ground splattered with spilled blood, littered with debris: an empty sandal, a green plastic bag, orange fruit spilling from it, a water bottle, a metallic bowl, chunks of cement. People returned with stories of a British man blown apart, of an absence of police, of seeing everything happen from a boat on the river, of holding each other in that boat in helpless disbelief as mayhem unfolded onshore.

But none of this was familiar to me. I hadn't seen it or heard it myself. Yet for some reason, every moment just before the wind hit my legs was now branded on my brain. I remember the young girl's eyes—large, round, and full of wounded pride when pushed aside by her sister. I remember we were at the foot of a long staircase and just behind us a holy man was standing several stairs up, posing for photos for two tourists. I remember feeling critical of this. I remember that the younger girl dropped one of her metallic instruments when bumped by her sibling. That we all searched for it around my wife's feet. I remember thinking the design unfolding on Lucie's hand was beautiful.

The rest is surrogate memory—photos, articles, stories that became placeholders, context makers, for an event that I was more part of than witness to, yet strangely still felt absent from.

Hidden away in our locked-down guesthouse room, we couldn't solve the conundrum of what to do next. There was no way we were going to venture out into the city to find a hospital, not with the potential of more bombs, not with the fear of what sort of hospital we might find. Yet as much as hunkering down in our room seemed like the only possible option, we were haunted by the unknown, by the possible risks we were taking by not seeking immediate care. Lying in bed, we tried to describe to each other how strange, how wrong our heads felt. Stuffed and empty, muffled and hollow, knocked-in and broken open, they held irreconcilable contradictions now.

The next morning, we climbed to the rooftop restaurant that overlooked the riverfront. The bathers were sparse, the ghats subdued, quiet, hesitant. A mounting wave of panic rose in me as we assessed our hearing in the peace of that morning. Ambient sounds, the clinking of silverware close by, the distant cries of birds, the ubiquitous thwack of wet laundry being beat against a rock, were all the same volume, as if they came from the same source. There was no depth to our perception of sound beyond the immediate vicinity. Some people's voices we could hear, others were just lips moving silently.

We bought last minute tickets home, despite our fears of what air travel, what waiting another 36 hours before seeing a doctor would do, perhaps irrevocably, to our ears. We prepared ourselves to venture forth through the labyrinth of alleyways once again, this time in the comfort, however illusory, of company. A Swedish couple would join us in finding a taxi to the airport. The man had briefly lost consciousness like we had. He frequently held his ear in much the same way. And they, like us, were fleeing Varanasi that morning. We would cluster together and make it to the main road as one.

But still we had doubts. The Swedes were continuing their vacation. Going to the beach in Goa to decompress, determined to forge ahead with their itinerary as if something life-changing had not just occurred. But our second-guessing was brief. Upon reaching the main road by foot and feeling our frayed nervous systems pulse and pound as we maneuvered the crossing of a typical Indian roadway, we realized without a doubt that we couldn't be there any longer. A road that just yesterday had been simply a road was now an endless negotiation of danger—of cows dragging maimed legs, of dogs' heads crushed beneath the wheels of auto-rickshaws.

Perhaps, under different circumstances, I would have cried once we reached a cruising altitude, safely on our way home. With the mad scramble of finding last minute flights, of alerting our friends and family that we were hurt but alive, of asking for help upon our return behind me, I would have truly let go. But Lucie was sick with what seemed like the first signs of food poisoning. She needed to go deeply interior to battle the nausea while she waited for the antibiotics we traveled with to take effect.

It was then, alone with my thoughts on that interminable flight, that I found myself unable to reconcile my feelings. Much like Varanasi itself, with its defiant refusal to separate opposites—beauty, horror, life, death, purity, filth, the holy, the profane, the noble, the petty—my mind spun out in endless iterations of gratitude and fear. I wondered about the girls' fate. Could they hear? Could they, two street children, expect any medical care, love, or community support? Were they even alive? Perhaps their bodies rested now next to that of the holy man, weighted down by stones at the bottom of the Ganges.

In this light, it seemed absurd to worry about Lucie and myself. We could walk. We could talk. We could see. We had each other. We had concerned family and friends mobilizing on our behalf at that very moment. We could afford to fly home and seek help. We were fortunate and privileged and so very lucky.

Nevertheless, these thoughts of gratitude clashed against a deep animal fear for our health. The flights home were quiet, but the silence for me was often loud and desperate. Sometimes it sounded like a distant washing machine deep within my head, or a thousand cash registers ringing up a sale just around the corner, or a neighbor shoveling snow, scraping the shovel against the sidewalk again and again with a relentless rhythm. Would I hear these sounds for the rest of my life? Was there even a treatment for whatever ailed us? Were we lucky, or unlucky?

In the end, it was this last question that haunted me the most, as if every event, every happening, could now be interpreted two ways. Perhaps this is what it meant to be stuck in the wheel of life and death, birth and rebirth. If my single head could contain all this, think of the Buddha's ears, how loud they must have rung, how strong his eardrums had to have been to sustain the noise and chatter of the suffering of the world. I recalled the scene where he battled his demons, taunting, petulant, mocking beasts full of schaden-freude, creatures full of hateful glee, trying anything to disturb the Buddha's equanimity. And then I thought of the puja ceremony we had run past, of those remarkable performers who continued to welcome the gods of the river despite the terror that swirled around them, their calm, synchronized move-ments a testament to their faith.

I tried my best to remain calm for Lucie during our long layover in Amsterdam. We found somewhere spacious for her to rest, to lie down amid our backpacks large and small. Alone again, I sought out an Internet café where more details of the bombing unspooled before me.

"Let's Feel the Pain Together" was the subject line of the e-mail by the Indian Mujahideen who claimed responsibility for the attack. They had tar-geted the Hindu puja ceremony as part of the ongoing power struggle be-tween Hindus and Muslims, as a retaliation for the destruction of the Babri Mosque by a mob of 150,000 Hindus that had literally torn the structure down to the ground.

The mastermind behind the Varanasi blast was thought to be a doctor in his mid-20s. The bomb detonated inside a plastic lunch box. The scent of henna was reported by the forensic unit investigating the material used. A 60-year-old pilgrim had succumbed to her injuries. A little girl had been intentionally abandoned by her family in the mayhem before they fled town.

I checked on my wife frequently. Abandoned to a deep, much-needed sleep, her body rested now much as it had amid the rubble. Thrown violently by a blast wind, or laid down gently of its own accord, the pose she assumed was eerily similar.

This unnerving coexistence of opposites began to separate out again as we arrived in Portland. Friends had arranged an appointment with the head of a hospital otolaryngology department shortly after our plane landed. There were no holy men or touts, no rivers somehow both filthy and pure, no orange flowers spilling from shrouded corpses on the cars in front of us as our taxi shuttled us from airport to hospital, from the doctor that bombed us to the one who would take care of our ears.

This world presented only one face. Whatever shadow it cast was kept out of sight.

We rushed into the hospital, late for our appointment, and bleary-eyed from two days of trauma and travel. We left our backpacks behind the secretary's desk and said our hasty goodbyes—a kiss, a squeeze of hands—as they ushered us to be examined separately.

Before I knew it, long conical devices were inserted deep within my ear canals, metallic clamps fastened against my skull behind my ears. I sat holding a small plastic box with a button I was instructed to push whenever I heard a sound, no matter how faint. A small stuffed animal, a smiling, black and white fluffy dog with its head cocked to the side, sat in a transparent plastic cube fastened to the wall in front of me. On either side of me were other dogs also in little plastic boxes bolted to the wall. Very different than the dogs of Varanasi, I thought, that skirted the very threshold of danger, that slept in roadways or nestled in the warm ashes of corpses. Dogs that could have been nestling right now in mine. Instead these toys were meant to calm and reassure young patients, children the same ages as the two little girls who had painted my wife's hands.

The testing proceeded. The audiologist scribbled her notes, gave instructions, and scribbled some more. I watched her every move, fearful she would disappear from her station behind the big glass window in front of me, and enter the room with the doctor, their faces solemn and stoic as they delivered the bad news.

By the time we reached the word-comprehension phase of the testing, I felt hopeless. The audiologist had released a white noise into my ears, like the diffuse rushing sound of an airplane mid-flight, or the static of a television left on long after the last show. Then she asked me to push the button at the first intimation of a sound and proceeded to play noises of various pitches that sounded like the whistling of distant fireworks, flying feebly, then dying just past the horizon.

Often I was sitting for what seemed like forever, without hearing anything at all beyond the shush of the white noise and the pulsing, whooshing sound my ears produced of their own accord. She must be playing sounds, I thought. She must. And with each added second of that white-noise silence, of my thumb sitting inactive atop the button in my hand, my hope shrank a little more. There was a whole world that I would now never hear. And I would now suffer sounds that no one else heard but me.

When it came time for the word-comprehension phase, I could no longer look at my audiologist's face through the pane of glass.

Say "home," her voice said, originating deep within my ears as if it were my own. "Home," I would say, eyes now closed. Say "king," she said, and the "king" I repeated felt feeble and weak. Say "numb," she said. My eyes spilled over with tears of deep, fearful exhaustion. "Numb," I said, a little louder than before. Say "love," she said, causing me to open my eyes. But the audiologist did not look up from her monitor.

"Love," I said, reminding myself that those horrible rhythmic sounds in the silence—the washing machine, the cash registers, the snow-shoveling neighbor in my head—those sounds were my heart. Those sounds in my head were my own heart beating. Those sounds in the silence were me, alive.

Lingua Familia

JUDITH ADKINS

Every family language is a mosaic of voiceprints.

Even the names of childhood pets tell. My brother and I called our cats Fluffy and Boots, the dogs Prince, Snoopy, and Rascal. My partner, R, and her brother named their cats Doodlezack Dodecahedron and Springerle Parallelopiped. Then came Sojourner Truth, Elizabeth Cady Stanton, and the one I knew as a wizened tomcat, Anthony B. Susan.

Every family language is a collage of utterances, each utterance a coming out.

My grandparents, German immigrants, learned English gradually through their children, who picked it up at school. Because Grandma and Grandpa continued to misspell words and misconstrue idioms, queer clichés made their way into the family argot. Chief among them: *You've got to take the bitter with the sweat.* Coming from our mouths, it shushed whiners and defused self-pity, hinting also at the sunbright-shadow helix of our household: all optimists or pessimists, nothing in between, coexisting.

Each family tongue bridges birthright family and chosen one, class-of-origin and class-of-aspiration, occupational roots and vocational branches, native cultural nexus and whatever context comes next. Echoing in it: ethnicity, education, place, and personality. Each family patois is a living thing, always evolving, always in flux, surprising even us—divided tongues like fire.

Because my father was a navy man, we spoke a kind of port language. From years on Oahu, *finished* was *pau*; after a stint on Guam, *underbrush* became *tangantangan*. Nautical confusions twisted our tongue. Dad said *stowage* instead of *storage* (then again, we were perpetually moving, at sea even on land, our storage more like stowage). The mottos of Admiral Hyman Rickover, father of the nuclear navy, echoed in our household. *Get with the program. Today is another day in which to excel.*

Lingua franca, another port tongue, was spoken along the eastern Mediterranean for centuries. Mostly Italian, with some French and Greek, Spanish and Turkish, Portuguese and Arabic mixed in, it eased trade and diplomacy, the get and the give of society. *Lingua franca* has a more general meaning as well: any mixed jargon bridging peoples. It's a common tongue—polyglot, shared, everyday—like the family tongue: *lingua familia.*

R's family recorded their sayings on a sheet of notebook paper, now yellowed and bespattered after years on the kitchen bulletin board. Some of these locutions emerged out of shared travels and adventures. Others were playful responses to the ambient tension felt in any household of imperfect spouses, childish children, mischievous pets. R's father, in youth a halting student, claimed that he graduated from college "*vix et aegri*" (barely and with difficulty): a family mantra repeated in the face of many a trial.

On Friday nights, after handing over car keys and money for a movie, my father would stand at the door and call after my brother and me, "Drive careful!"

"*Ly*! Drive careful*ly*!" we'd cry back, half smart-alecky, half-ashamed of Dad's residual twang, and his failure to master the adverb. Our cover blown, despite fine schools—our origins made known.

Soon after I turned 15, we moved to Scotland, where my teachers and schoolmates spoke with an accent so thick it seemed a different language. That brogue, that burr, more music than speech, rolled in my ears, left me at sea. I couldn't understand it much of the time, grew weary of asking "*What?*" and lost the ability to speak in class. My words careened off cinderblock; my voice turned too many right angles; my otherness resounded: an outsider who couldn't pass, an American, a military kid linked to the town's controversial base. (On the streets, protestors blared:

"Tell the Yanks! To shove it down the stanks! We didnae want Polaris!")
Maybe also my body knew, deep down where will begets sound, that other
things about me were askew. I couldnae spaek.

In every family, what you don't-ask-don't-tell. Keep stowed away. A heavy
hollow to carry. A lowering cloud of white space, hovering.

Throughout my childhood, I read the feature in my mother's *Ladies' Home
Journal* called "Can This Marriage Be Saved?" Each month a husband and
wife told his-and-her stories of marital strife, and a therapist offered
advice. Feeling superior, I grasped what Steve and Barb, Ted and Jane,
and all their kind evidently could not: the underlying problem was always
the same, and such a simple one, too. "Communication!" I'd sneer to anyone
willing to listen.

As an adolescent, I modified this assessment: the crux of the problem was the
gulf of gender. Being a lesbian, it seemed, meant avoiding this difficulty
altogether, meant never needing a man to understand. No Mars versus Venus
for me. I felt a ripple of guilt for copping out of that ancient noble struggle,
then a wave of relief. No I'm-a-Woman-Talking-to-a-Man sense of standing
outside the self, working the levers of that cranky old machine. In addition, I
thought, two women conversing, all gender differences stripped away, might
offer an ideal of intimate communication. Just two people in a room. One self
talking to another self.

My native argot is remarkable for misspoken words and mangled grammar,
plus terms and inflections picked up in one home port or another. In homage
to our Scottish sojourn, we goofed the pronunciation of *books*, rhyming it
with *spooks*. R's family patois, resplendent with Latin and Biblical allusion,
seemed sophisticated by comparison. "It's the eschaton!" her parents would
exclaim when she cleaned her room.

A longtime friend, one of my chosen Family, tells me things are going well
with her new girlfriend but mentions that they have different conversational
cadences, and I feel an inner sinking, thinking about what women together
are like, worrying that all forms of intercourse—talking, kissing, etcetera—

interrelate, that being out of phase in one portends mismatch in others, and recall some kissers in my past: too darting or peripheral, hesitant to go there, deaf to my body's silent entreaty—*commit the tongue already.*

From the moment I met R, I wanted her tongue. She understood *ontology*, *ontogeny*, and *teleology*. I could never keep them straight; she could explain all with bracing clarity. Even *deontology* and *soteriology*. It's true, what they say, that you gravitate to some other who has what you seek: in my case, a surer faith, a clearer sense of vocation, a more intellectual life, and a richer lexicon. I wanted to drink the wine of her language—mine so thin in comparison.

IN HER KISS I TASTE THE REVOLUTION
(a Lesbian Avengers poster the decade we met)

Words were at the heart of our courtship. We road-tripped around New England, hiked mountains, made complicated meals in tiny kitchens, all while playing word games of our own invention:

The Half-Known Word Game. One player offers up a word she claims to only half-understand, like *autochthonous* or *exoteric*; the other tries to figure out whether half-ignorance is feigned or genuine.

The Zeugma Game. Players make up sentences containing a zeugma, a figure of speech in which a verb or adjective is applied jointly to two or more words in a different sense. For example: "The tree towered over our house, as Father did over our childhood."

The New York Times *Challenge Game.* Players suggest a word or phrase neglected by the general public and then use it widely and often until it starts appearing in a major newspaper. We're still working on *pons asinorum.*

Other diversions: Imaginary-Word Scrabble, the Word-by-Word Collaborative Sermon-Writing Game, the Non Sequitur Game, the Fictitious Academic Conference Title Game. All were foreplay to the labor of merging lives, of creating another.

When R gave birth, we gave our son, S, my last name coupled with hers. In a golden glaze of fatigue and euphoria, we saw it on the birth certificate in black typeface: Adkins-Hooke. This, of all things, broke me up—that a new human had my name, and that the Commonwealth of Virginia was letting us get away with it: a homofuse. For a generation at least, our identities would be linguistically linked. My two syllables, plus her one, beat a decent rhythm, and we each bring a *k* to echo the other's. Yet I've never liked the *dk* mashup at my syllable break—too much clatter at once, plus that awkward seesaw of tongue. Not to mention, the transition from my *s* to her *h* isn't great. Say our names together and there's work involved, clumsiness, uncertainty about whether you're going to get there.

The gay lexicon of the 1990s, when I finally owned up to being Family, included the fierce cries of Queer Nation—*We're Here, We're Queer, Get Used To It!*—and Act Up's stark equations: *Silence=Death*. A decade later, when our lives had zoomed in from street and public square to home and childcare, we—a smaller family—still took up those slogans, repurposing them. When the basement flooded: *We're Here, We're Queer, We're Cleaning Our Basement!* When the baby slept after a long crying jag: *Silence=Bliss*. Each utterance was a dissonant chord, accompanied by a half-smile, half-grimace—that we and these words had come to this.

The closest I've come to having A Song with someone was Lucinda Williams's "Something About What Happens When We Talk," associated with a former love, now tender friend. Our relationship, mostly long-distance with a rhythm of visits, was stripped to essentials. For a spell, all words and no body. *Conversation with you was like a drug*. Then two people in a room. No words and all body. Stripped down, back then.

Today S and I are in a room. He asks questions and I try to answer: the call and response of child and parent. *Why isn't one a prime number? Are boomerangs scary? What's a griffin?* I play ten rounds of What Time Is It Mr. Fox, clean up a potion of pulverized tortilla and wild strawberries, construct a leprechaun trap from a shoebox, forked stick, polished stone, miniature golden sabre. When the beautiful mess overwhelms us, R's wry refrain (borrowed from songstress Carole King): *Life is a tapestry of rich and royal hue*.

Every once in a while, I utter some term unknown to R. *Newel post*, for example. Gloating over my tiny verbal victory, I fabricate reasons to say it.

"Well, I think I'll just hang my jacket on this *newel post*." *Newel*: from the French for kernel, for stone. *Newel post*: that vertical at the top or bottom of a stair railing, an upright on the margins, something you can grasp in between. As a child, I hovered there at the threshold, eavesdropping, sifting for kernels of adult truth, amazed to discover that my parents' voices, in assumed privacy, shifted in pitch and timbre. A different language without me there?

Our son's father teaches German language and literature but sometimes wishes he'd become a linguist. On the floor of his study, we make S a "hamster nest," a makeshift bed of pillows and quilts. Bookcases looming overhead hold Turkish and Icelandic dictionaries, tapes of Dutch and Finnish, a box of Greek vocabulary cards. *Pimsleur's Persian* abuts *Continuing with Russian*; an American Sign Language dictionary nestles up with a Sanskrit one. Snuggling down into his nest, S looks up at *Extinct Languages* and *Suffix Obsession* and *Harri Potter a Maen yr Athronydd*. When I say goodnight, he answers, "Unka goon."

"What does that mean?"

"Good night. In hamster language."

The next generation—expanding the family patois—divided tongues like fire.

A family tic, which I'm embarrassed to admit: how R and I quote or riff on Virginia Woolf, reflecting too predictably who we are (White Women of A Certain Age w/ Creative Interests + Designer-Brand Education). Yet certain references from *To The Lighthouse* haunt our house, irresistible, essential to survival:

Someone had blundered. (Echoing Tennyson's "The Charge of the Light Brigade," Woolf signals that an affront has been made to the fragile ego of her book's patriarch, Mr. Ramsay.)

He would never reach R. (Mr. Ramsay comes up against his limits: "For if thought . . . like the alphabet is ranged in 26 letters all in order, then his splendid mind had no sort of difficulty in running over those letters one by one, firmly and accurately, until it had reached, say, the letter Q. He reached Q. . . . But after Q?")

A story spawning a family expression came to us from our son's father, who heard it from our son's godmother. A researcher visiting an archive in England went through a long process to gain admission: identification was proffered, forms completed, a carrel assigned. When the researcher asked to use the restroom, she was told to give up her carrel and repeat the entry process.

"But I just did all that," she protested.

"Well, then," the room monitor replied in his stiff accent, "I'm afraid you've inconvenienced yourself."

We've inconvenienced ourselves: a convenient refrain, a comic balm for the pain of living with the consequences of decisions and actions. Especially if one has embraced certain overarching inconveniences to self: committing to another, having a child.

When S was three, he fell off a stool and bit down hard on his tongue, slicing a gash across perfect pink. The nurse on call advised no special care. "The tongue heals itself," she said. "It's miraculous." My own tongue, partly paralyzed since those adolescent years in Scotland, was suddenly healed by parenthood. Loss of self brought also a loss of self-consciousness. I could speak in groups again. Miraculous—how family takes away, how it gives, at once.

When I'm on the phone, R can tell if I'm speaking to my parents. I give myself away by tone, a monosong of cheer, glossing the way I feel: overwhelmed by this life of rich and royal hue, also desperate to realize My Potential, to make up for lost time, the years passing like paragraphs. I don't consciously shape my inflection but know R perceives something real: my lungs, lips, and tongue won't permit my parents to hear from their child, their youngest offspring, any jangling notes of disappointment, regret, midlife panic. This particular voice is a piano with a too-bright action, protecting them and masking my shame. Now, not so many more days in which to excel before my paragraphs conclude. I will never reach Q.

Family is a linguistic construct: call yourselves one and you become. Call a boy your son, yourself a mother, and you both become one to the other. R is *Mommy*; I am *Mama*, a name at first resisted (calling to mind rose water and housedresses), then embraced (chiming for years now in my son's sweet voice). Still, on occasion some other moniker takes shape in sound, calling out the queerness of me in the lexicon of family. At the playground kids flock around, but they're uncertain what to make of a boyish woman, a mashup, willing to run, climb, and chase. When we stop to catch our breath, a child in pigtails and pink dress stares at me hard and asks, "Are you a boy? Or a girl?"

"I'm a woman," I reply. She looks unconvinced. "What about *you*?" I ask. "Are you a girl, or a boy?"

"A *girl*," she huffs, indignant.

We start the chase again.

"Monster Daddy! Monster Daddy!" the girl starts calling me, and the name takes.

Each family tongue is esoteric; it's a ghetto lingo that coheres your few and excludes others. At the same time, every family tongue is *exoteric*— "comprehensible to or suited to the public"—because household dialects share certain general features: a complex syntax of ringing silences, a smattering of homegrown jargon, a steady thrum of pressure-release humor. The specifics may be private, but the whole is a lingua franca recognizable to all: that bridge, that rickety one, between intimates.

Each family has its network of treacherous conversational roadways, the merge onto one sometimes obscured: a surprise following a blind curve. IKEA furniture, say. An enormous bookcase. Five types of screws, two kinds of dowels, two twisty things not quite screws, one hex wrench. A cacophony of wooden planes. Not one word to direct assembly, only drawings of a cartoon figure going through the motions. I stare at the pictures blankly, paralyzed. R sighs, "Come *on*. You're part *Swedish*." I sit inert, helpless. Sighing again, she declares, "I wish I had a girlfriend who liked to put things together." A pierce. It stings. I pull back my bow-string—"I wish *I* had a girlfriend who . . . ," my voice taut, quivering. A rush then to mutual apology and we agree: nothing good can come of a sentence starting that way. We delete it from the lexicon, falling back on an old sacred vow: "Friendship pact." R and I exchange the phrase, shake on it, and quietly, *vix et aegri*, build our case.

In hamster language, according to S, "to cowder" means "to get warm, but not from, like, a furnace, from something else, like, snuggling." I think: cower, chowder, cow dear, things bovine and contained, warm milk and clean hay, a boy curled up in a barn, trying to feel safe.

A *pons asinorum*, combining the Latin for *bridge* and *ass*, is "a problem that severely tests the ability of an inexperienced person" or "a critical test of ability or understanding: STUMBLING BLOCK." A useful term. Consider, for example, family life. More than any other context, it throws us upon each other (our sharp knees, our neuroses, crowded together). In its dense paragraph of shared time and space, we feel our way through the *tangantangan* of relation, the conundrum of each child, the fatigue of the daily drill, the frailty of the body. It's a critical test of ability and understanding. Many have stumbled.

An opener that tells: *I love you very much, but . . .* , always followed by a direct criticism. Thus, we mercifully proffer a shield and then let one small arrow fly.

Certain utterances become water under the bridge. For example, after I came out—rolling the family ship, deviating from the program—my mother wrote me a letter. Her words stung then but have long since been forgiven. At the end of our phone conversations these days, we give an extra embrace to the closing clichés—*I love you, I love you too, Thanks for calling, You're welcome*—as if the musical score of these measures were marked *con forza*: tiny vocal crests set in motion by undercurrents of, perhaps, *I'm sorry* and *I understand* and *We are all getting old, none of that matters now*.

One year in my 20s, I lived mostly off my voice, raising money for a gay rights organization and conducting surveys for a polling firm. *Will you give $50 to help end hate crimes? In your opinion, is the economy getting worse, getting better, about the same?* To keep a person on the phone, I mirrored pace and tone. Young New Yorkers required a certain rhythm and inflection, Southwest retirees another. Sometimes the person on the line would try to anchor me geographically. "Where do you *think* I'm from?" I'd ask. The top guess: California, perhaps a catchall for anyone with a subtle accent or none at all. Yet it was curious, given the many ports of my childhood, to have my voice linked with one I've never called home. *My* voice? That rootless, shifting soundscape.

Over time, R and I have come to sound alike. On the phone, everybody thinks one is the other. Maybe this happens to most couples: the result when two intimates match cadences and mirror tones, intermarry vocabularies and spawn new ones. Maybe, instead, this is a peculiarity of same-sex love, most evident in couples without gender difference there to maintain a defensive octave between voices. I wanted to merge tongues, yes, but now our own mothers can no longer distinguish us. Someone had blundered.

Being gay has long invited wordplay: the necessary invention of terms for lovers and love acts without a name, for new bodies, genders, and sexualities. Ambisextrous bois. Pangender faeries. Trysexual trykes. Linguistic flexibility and creativity a part of the history: the inheritance. Now many who are Family are becoming husbands, becoming wives: marital bonds entwine queer tongues. Oh camerados.

The conversation I imagined in the solitude of my mind was a clean progression of sound and sense. However, face to face, brown eye to deep brown eye, the words shuffled, muddled, snagged. Each statement clanged a reprove; each request shrilled like a blame. Not the clarinet's open tones but the pinch of an oboe instead. Two women in a room. Her face before me. Not the sculpted marble I must have envisioned, but living flesh, a thousand thoughts and feelings moving in it. I couldnae spaek.

Silence=Death (a kind of). Or Silence=Life (a kind of, or the one as you know it).

If I could give you three things, I would give you these.
Song and laughter and a wooden home in the shining seas.
R sings Gordon Bok's "Isle au Haut Lullaby" to S at bedtime, to me when I'm anxious.

Do you hear what the sails are saying in the wind's dark song?
Give sadness to the wind, blown alee and gone.
It comforts me more than any other song.
Sleep now the moon is high, and the wind blows cold,
For you are sad and young, and the sea is old.
There's something about that weave of mysterious sorrow and simple joy, infinite ocean and particular home, transient life and ancient world. It's what I want to hear when I'm all *pau*. "Sing me 'Isle au Haut' on my deathbed," I've asked R jokingly, seriously. She's given her word.

Two women in a room, speaking across a canyon. Between the words, ambiguous silences. The products of confusion? Compassion? Cowardice? Of thoughts too embryonic or unruly to find form in language? Each quiet space is far from mute, each a shifting kaleidoscope: the shapes and colors of meaning colliding, rearranging, impossible to get a fix on. As the conversation ends without resolution—the way forward a blank and a tangle—an honest exchange: "I'm glad we talked."

I'm on the porch of the family cabin in Maine. R and S are inside, talking. Their voices filter through the walls. The goldenrod is blooming. Penobscot Bay stretches before me. His tones are excitable and chirping, hers deeper and smoother. Both are muffled, merging. The sky blurs into milky blue bay. A meld, a melt. I can't tell what they're saying. The sound is utterly familiar, completely incomprehensible. Both qualities are key to the pleasure I take in it. Dissonance and song from this wooden home in this shining sea. I love the voices of my family, love them best at a slight remove.

The call and response of parent and child. Children parrot the family idiom, showing what you habitually say. S begins declarations with "The thing about me is . . . ," which we recognize instantly. How often this crosses our lips, how desperate we must be to assert individuality. *You need to know: I am this way.* Our son has the words on the tip of his tongue, the idea in his mind: the self-in-family is precarious—requires vigilant defense.

Autochthonous: "formed or originating in the place where found."

"No . . . children never forget. For this reason, it was so important what one said, and what one did, and it was a relief when they went to bed": the thoughts of Mrs. Ramsay in *To the Lighthouse*, also my thoughts in my house.

My family-of-origin speaks best through gesture, movement, action. On a bank beside a river, during a Mother's Day picnic, I play Frisbee with my nephew. My brother joins in, then my sister-in-law, finally my parents, rising stiffly from the two lawn chairs. Our family circle forms a circle and saucers across it a bright yellow ring, asterisking the invisible spot in the center equidistant from all of us. My father stretches down his long arm to pluck up a fallen Frisbee, no bending more than necessary, then throws like a pro. My brother miscalculates, grazes Mom, runs over to touch her arm. My nephew karate kicks to catch the ring with his toe, then clops it on his buzz-cut head like a halo. For an hour, our motion is communication, our only words mantras of apology and praise. *I'm sorry! My fault! Good one! Well done!* Midgame we agree: apology for the bad throws we make is understood, unnecessary. Nobody mutes the compliments. Three generations launch forth invisible filaments, ever unreeling them, ever tirelessly speeding them, till the bridge we will need be formed, while the river beside us rushes on to the falls.

"Stop talking!" S demands one day in the middle of a snuggle.
"Why?"
"Because!"
"Because why?"
"Because the snuggling is better if you don't talk."

Warehouse

OLIVIA WOLFGANG-SMITH

O ur professor's written directions to New York's Attica Correctional Facility have a flair for the dramatic. Clutched in my slightly trembling fist, they tell us that the prison's walls will "loom" on our left to signal the final turn. But loom they do, solid and menacing in the half-light of the winter evening, almost inconceivably big compared to the three bleak hours of interstate my classmate and I have passed through. This is open, distant country, farms and mountains and oasis villages nestled in dips in the rocky soil. The prison is a high-walled, turreted exception, an industrial edifice that looks like it has wandered from its urban home and lost itself in the woods.

I am already a mess, wound impossibly tight. My driving companion—fraternity guy, lacrosse athlete—appears unruffled. Our shared English major seems the only thing we have in common. "We're early," he says. "Wanna eat?" I do. So we coast past the prison, the state flag flopping weakly on its pole, the sprawling parking lot that suggests an amusement park more than anything else. I was raised rural—this much asphalt signals a vacation somehow, a deviation from the norm.

It makes sense that the building itself is big. It is maximum security, over maximum capacity, full to the brim with men siphoned in for violent crimes or for infractions committed at other correctional facilities.

America is a nation of prisons; 2.4 million of us locked up, seven times the incarceration rate of western Europe. Incarceration is built into our national heritage, particularly by the nineteenth-century Quakers' hopeful vision for a true penitentiary. This utopian facility, first attempted with the establishment of Eastern State Penitentiary in Philadelphia in 1829, would theoretically use solitude and reflection to scrub clean the criminal soul, while still conveying in its architecture "a cheerless blank indicative of the misery that awaits the unhappy being who enters." The Quakers' carceral method was one of total solitary confinement, with prisoners masked and hooded for trips outside their solid-walled cells in order to avoid visual contact between inmates. Each convict was provided with a Bible. The philosophy supporting this warehouse was that time spent in complete solitude and religious contemplation would eventually rouse the criminal's conscience and render him penitent.

We have long warehoused each other, and this imposing fortress is among our most infamous warehouses. Attica has loomed here since 1931, discontent rising by degrees until it boiled over into an inmate rebellion in September, 1971. My father was 14 when he watched the news coverage of the uprising—the inmates seizing control of D Yard, taking correctional officers hostage. Negotiating for their rights to worship, read, and bathe, some of them hoping for amnesty, they were met with silence from Governor Nelson Rockefeller—until he phoned in the order for the National Guard and state troopers to retake the facility, blanketing D Yard with tear gas and opening fire into the resulting fog for two uninterrupted minutes. Thirty-nine men were killed by gunfire in the retaking of the prison, including ten hostages.

In the decades since, America's memory of the uprising has faded. I am a product of these years of collective forgetting. Even now, staring down the physical fact of the prison itself, I find the first association in my head is not Rockefeller, nor the ricochet of bullets and stinging gas, but Al Pacino—all butterfly collar and Bronx accent, the rasping scream of "Attica!" in *Dog Day Afternoon*. I have researched the uprising, memorized its statistics, watched the original news coverage—seen footage of broadcasts "at the scene" in the very parking lot we are cruising past now, reporters gulping with emotion as the Doppler-distorted buzz of helicopters rends the air. But still, in open defiance of my efforts to learn this history of my adopted state, Pacino's character shouts down the actual uprising in my mind.

But Attica is still Attica. The building before me is an aggregate of intimidation and wrongdoing; it overwhelms on sight. My breathing shallows. I am glad when my classmate and I turn the corner, though I know we will be back.

The prison overshadows the town that shares its name. The diner we stop in is dusky inside and deserted. Shards of fuselage from a wrecked BMX bike are arranged behind glass, a memorial to the local high schooler who died on it. I wonder what it must be like to grow up here, how far Atticans have to travel before they can announce their hometown with relaxed shoulders, without fear of a joke or grimace. My classmate and I sit in the indoor twilight and eat sandwiches thick with shredded iceberg lettuce, while he makes polite conversation and my brain spins its wheels.

This is new, this feeling. It's not that I'm a confident person. Actually, I'm adept at being nervous. Over the years I've gotten almost paradoxically comfortable with it—learned to surf the feeling, use it to my advantage. But today I am confronted by something new. My classmate and I are studying Prison Writing at our east-coast hilltop bubble of a college, our professor a social activist in a fedora and cardigan, and we have driven these three hours to sit in on the creative writing workshop he runs for about a dozen of the inmates.

I enrolled in this class eagerly, and I have devoured our readings with the enthusiasm and social righteousness of the young and privileged. But in the past few days, I have been shocked to discover that I am in fact terrified of the prison visit itself. For one thing, I am a student of creative writing, not psychology; I am not used to confronting my human subjects openly. And there's something instinctive and prehistoric in me that considers the idea of a secure space meant to house only dangerous people, and concludes over and over again *Don't go in there.* This is not the wall I belong behind.

Back at the prison, my classmate parks us nose-forward in that expanse of a lot.

"Here we go!" He offers a smile that I am physically incapable of returning.

Before we left campus, I spent the morning trying to regulate my mood—drinking coffee to perk up, listening to gentle music to calm down, zoning out until friends were uncertain if it was safe to leave me alone in public. It is like I have forgotten how to be me, how to perform Olivia. I am just a thing, full of caffeine and Leonard Cohen, about to confront a group of men who have not left this building in years, perhaps decades. Some who never will. My brain is overheating trying to prepare for a situation for which it has no useful data. Yes, I am nervous.

Passing through the facility's main gates feels harder than it should, like getting on an escalator without looking. Inside we meet our fedora'd professor and begin our journey to the classroom. The hat—which our professor doesn't yet remove, as though a signal that we're not fully Inside—is familiar and thus comforting. It is a scrap of collegiate life that, like my classmate's polo, is strange to see transposed to this setting. I wonder if I look as out of place. I hope I do.

Correctional officers in short-sleeved uniforms size us up. These men are brusque with us, run ragged by this career, their local industry—a job that journalist Ted Conover calls "a life sentence in eight-hour shifts." One takes my driver's license and files it out of sight behind a long counter. I swallow the mounting panic that comes with being stripped of identity. In response to a combination of the guard's uniform and his expression, I feel instantly and vaguely guilty, like a teenager caught loitering. I remove my glasses to pass through a metal detector; skittish, I scramble for them on the other side. By the time I blink my vision clear again, my classmate has followed me through without incident and is standing unflappable beside me, affable hands in khaki pockets.

"Good job," our professor says quietly. There is mild relief in his voice—perhaps the anxiety of the shepherd, grateful that his street-stupid Little Ivy contingent has made it inside without causing a scene. But he also flashes understanding—an acknowledgment of the glares from the guards, of the clammy, niggling sensation that we are not fully welcome here. That this place is not for us, not for daytrip visits by the curious and civic-minded. This place is meant to stay with you and you with it.

The prison is less intimidating from within, taken room by room, but it still has the uneasy vibe of the institutional. We walk briskly through low-ceilinged, over-polished corridors, turning at central hubs until I lose all sense of direction. At each junction there are more guards—keying open grated doors, radioing ahead to warn of our approach, stamping and checking our hands. It is the most policed I have ever been.

I am made conspicuous by my gender. The volunteers we've met, the correctional officers, the unseen inmates stored down each hallway—all are men. I do not feel threatened, but still the realization breaks over me like a sweat. I am determined not to buckle under it, not to consider myself alone here in any sense. I am inspired in this venture by my classmate, who seems as at-ease here as in our college's female-dominated English seminars—classrooms in which he is often the only male voice. His flat refusal to be nervous impresses me, but I can't quite follow—can't convince myself that it doesn't matter to be so thoroughly unfamiliar here.

As we walk, our professor narrates in a low voice: here the daily medications are doled out; here gates screen the entrance to the infamous D Yard; here a gloomy corridor leads to the cellblocks. Every new stretch of hallway is deserted but for the guards stationed at its end—a fact that my professor seems as uncertain of as I am before we round each corner. He remarks casually on the absence of inmates. I am wondering where they are, when they will appear. I am remembering to breathe.

The classroom looks like an elementary-school library about to be renovated. Concrete and tile lend a stale chill to the air; a few odd books rest on shelves and counters. I am surprised to see that the walls are covered in murals—scenes of life in the Great Camps of the Adirondacks, a hunting lodge aesthetic of trees and waterfalls and occasional deer. I can't decide if the murals strike me as kind or taunting. The desks are attached to their chairs, as in grade school, and at our professor's direction, my classmate and I arrange them in a shallow semi-circle. He deposits his hat and coat in the corner and moves to write the next week's assignment on the board. I choose a chair-desk and wait, chewing the inside of my cheek.

Muffled sounds seep in from the hallway and before I can think of what to do with myself, the men arrive.

The men arrive. They arrive at once, just under a dozen of them, and though I am not scared, neither am I comfortable. They are clean-cut, friendly—by every logical definition, unintimidating. And yet I am intimidated, because my brain is determined to be—as determined as the men themselves are to be approachable.

Most of them are middle-aged. Their haircuts are precise, their beards kempt. Laugh lines web the corners of their eyes. Work colleagues, neighbors, family friends. They shake our hands and smile, give their names, lean forward to hear mine stammered in return. "Nice to meet you," they say. "Thanks for coming." Their clothes are state-issued, all in shades of green, but their shoes are individual and well cared for. One man, who is well over six feet tall and sports a full white beard, wears wingtips and earth-toned argyle socks. He shakes hands with my frat-brother classmate but gives me a smiling nod instead, pulls over another desk rather than filling in the remaining empty seat next to mine. He has, it seems, read the intensity in my expression, the youth and femaleness of me, and offered in response the gesture of keeping a careful distance. I will learn later that he is a model inmate, a gardener, a cook, allowed the relative freedom of a cell in the honor block. I will learn too that he was once an enforcer for a biker gang. By the end of the night I will wish that he had felt comfortable enough to shake my hand.

I have come expecting the radically different and instead am confronted with the familiar; my brain skips in this groove for the first several minutes of class. One by one, the men shake hands with our professor. They exchange smiles rich with honest affection, water-cooler greetings, the shy excitement of bookish friends about to begin a favorite class. Beats of introductory humor sound through the hum of my panic: one man sees that next week's assignment—from Phillip Lopate's anthology *The Art of the Personal Essay*, their course textbook—is Walter Benjamin's "Hashish in Marseilles" and quips, "That's what I'm talking about." When our professor forgets that he has already greeted one inmate and moves to shake his hand again, another says of his comrade, "You're invisible! It's a wonder you even ended up in prison!" I laugh, too hard, and it's not my laugh—it sounds like I'm still learning how. The men look at me with wry smiles, and I feel like a drunk at a church basement supper.

Then the class begins in earnest. My brain, recognizing the familiar patterns of a liberal arts seminar, turns over and kicks back in. We workshop some of the inmates' writing—first a short story that takes place largely on the move, its young protagonists driving through the streets of Buffalo. A love letter to a run-down rust bucket of a city. We transition to a personal essay from the argyle-socked gardener, meditating on his relationships with various volunteers and guards—the kindly, the cruel, the treacherously indifferent. He links his prison garden and the food he grows there to the other adventures that patch of ground has seen—the stabbings; the countless silent struggles for selfhood; and once, before his stewardship, the state-ordered gunfire that still echoes for Attica's current residents, inmate and correctional officer alike. Listening to his piece, I get the sense that within Attica there's a kind of unofficial ancestry to the story of the 1971 uprising—it's as though these men consider themselves blood descendants of the inmates killed that September; as though the guards patrolling outside our classroom door feel that their own fathers were the ones taken hostage.

And the writing is good. The writing is great. These men have applied to get into this class—which does nothing towards making them eligible for parole—on the strength of their writing samples. They have waited for spots to open, for the chance to cultivate an intellectual life behind bars. They have earned this, and they are using it. I am scrawling notes as though taking dictation, struggling to keep up. I realize this and my pen slows to a covert, guilty pace, my eyes determinedly not on my notebook. I feel the shame of an ill-suited field reporter or anthropologist—too conscious of the taking of evidence, the scribbled, impersonal collection of the comments and lives of these men.

When I stop writing I notice that the men are listening thoughtfully as their classmates read aloud, and that their feedback is heavily supportive. Again and again they ask each other for more—another paragraph of description, another city block's worth of narrative in a driving scene. They wonder, tactfully, if another tone or metaphor might fit a given passage more smoothly. I am listening, nodding, saying undergraduate creative writer things like, "In some ways it seems like the city of Buffalo is the real central character here." The author gives a small smile, nods his thanks. I am forgetting that he accesses Buffalo exclusively in memory.

They listen intently to our professor's input, pencils poised. They are as eager for his critique as for his praise. There is a mutual respect to the conversation between them, inmate and professor, two writers. This room is full of enthusiasm for the work, academia stripped of its posturing and pretension. And yet there's something that takes its place in the air, a kind of tension—a desperation. The men are wringing everything out of this workshop not only because they enjoy it, but because it is all there is. The memories of this evening of intellectual engagement will have to last them two weeks, while my classmate, my professor, and I juggle our countless other projects, the commitments we have chosen to make. Perhaps for the first time, I begin to see that juggling as privilege.

As a workshop we discuss Seneca's "On Noise," an ancient "moral epistle" in which the Stoic argues that distraction comes not from outside agitation but from inner turmoil. The essay begins, "I cannot for the life of me see that quiet is as necessary to a person who has shut himself away to do some studying as it is usually thought to be," a claim that resonates with chilling irony here. The men find Seneca's argument interesting, but ultimately quaint and something less than useful, coming as it does from a man who had to contend with living "right over a public bathhouse" but not with lockdowns and lights out and cellblock neighbors. Overcoming inner turmoil does not change the fact that external forces dictate the rhythms of these men's lives, and they must find a way to live and work within those constraints. "If I want quiet to write," one muses, "I usually wake up around three or four. That's the sweet spot."

I start in surprise at his comment, recalling suddenly where I am. Despite the reality of the prison around us, it is disconcertingly easy to forget that these men are here for a reason. I assumed I would be battling a consciousness of their crimes at every moment; instead I am half lulled into believing that I could leave the classroom and stroll across campus to my dorm.

I recognize that this is not a random sampling of inmates—that these men are artists, and that they have had decades inside to gain control, sober up, find themselves. But the selves they have found are so complexly aware of their own failures. They are using their writing to work toward the reflection and rehabilitation that the Quakers hoped could be accomplished through social and sensory deprivation.

As a creative writing student, I too have spent years cultivating a sense of self founded on writing. Now I find myself sitting in a room full of men who share my deepest interest, who speak intelligently and eloquently about literature I find interesting, and who have also committed violent and terrible crimes. I am struggling to pin down exactly where to draw the line between us, and that leaves me shaken.

A bell rings, and it is during the final round of thank-yous and goodbyes that I locate that line between us at last. As the inmates shake off the temporary indulgence of their earnest smiles for the return to the cellblock, I recognize their motivation for writing only as it is carefully masked by their new prison-blank expressions: they are writing against that blankness, against being forgotten; writing against being smudged from the world's memory as neatly as their inmate ancestors have been in the years since 1971. They are writing against the forces that make the rest of us forget those we send away, writing to assert themselves against the ways pop culture represents them. In every happy, helpful, desperate moment of the workshop, these men have been battling against their pasts and against the prison itself, toward rehabilitation, toward a different understanding of themselves and the lives they have led, the choices they have made. They have not given up on themselves, though others have. These grown men, these intellectuals, these writers, are negotiating for scraps of power over their own lives and legacies. This is a power that I don't have to ask for. It is my right, as a citizen of the Outside.

I walk faster.

And then here we are in the fresh chill of Outside, standing under the halogen streetlamps that light the parking lot, looking at the frosty clouds of our vital breath and flapping arms, snapping fingers against the cold. It is over, for us. I am exhausted by the release of residual pressure, sucking in air as if surfacing.

My classmate and I take a moment in the parked car to regroup. At last we are on the same page, having both been set on our heels. "Wow," he says, and I nod.

In the weeks to come I will find myself crying, suddenly and without warning, for about ten seconds at a time. Each time it will stop as abruptly as it starts. At first I will fail to explain this—to others, to myself. But eventually I will recognize a pattern and realize that I am being moved to tears by the act of opening doors, of coming and going as I please. Tramping across campus for coffee in the morning. Trudging up the hill to the library for a forgotten book. Holding the keys to my own shoebox dorm room and its popsicle-stick furniture.

But for now, closing my own car door, I simply feel enormously power-ful—the world before me terribly, wonderfully complex. We rest a moment, gearing up for the highway. And then we are gone.

Dirty Laundry

R O B E R T L O N G F O R E M A N

returned to my apartment in Athens, Ohio, at the end of a summer spent elsewhere, to find in my closet someone's dirty laundry. In a black garbage bag were two pairs of panties, a bra, a tank top, some shirts, a black skirt, and a pair of long socks.

Sarah, a young woman from Leipzig, had subleased the one-bedroom unit in my absence. She had moved out the day before I returned. She must have put the clothes in the closet and forgotten them, I thought; they certainly weren't left there for me. We had not been lovers, or friends. We had barely ever spoken—never about our personal lives, nor about our underwear—but now, unlikely as it seemed, I was in possession of her underwear. I could do whatever I wanted with them. I could wear them or sell them and she wouldn't know.

Rather than do these things, at least at first, I left the clothes as they were and wrote about them in my diary. I wrote, "It's almost as though she's still here. Something of her still hangs in the air, the air she breathed in July. It will haunt me until the day I leave, and I cannot take these clothes with me when I move out." I was right about that last part. I would have to do something with Sarah's clothes, but in part because I had never owned women's clothing, I didn't know what to do with them.

I knew I could throw the clothes away, but effort and money had been spent to create and then acquire them, so I felt it would have been wasteful to consign them to a landfill. I asked my women friends—I knew no drag queens—if they might like a free skirt or shirt. No one wanted them, though, or they doubted Sarah's clothes would fit, so the bag remained where Sarah had left it, most of the time.

A month after I found Sarah's long, discarded socks among her other things, I put them on. I didn't think the socks would be sexually arousing to wear, or emotionally fulfilling, but I had never worn such lengthy socks and I was curious to know what I'd been missing for 23 years. They were thick and made of a fabric I couldn't name. They were the first women's clothes ever to interest me without at the time being worn or taken off by a woman.

They fit well and reached higher than my knees, but they didn't belong on my feet. Their off-white color didn't suit my skin tone—and it felt, as I pulled each one over an ankle, like I was doing something wrong, and not only because I had always worn shorter socks. My interest in Sarah's clothes had gone too far. It was as though when I adorned myself with the forfeited garments I had put on vestigial pieces of Sarah, as if she should feel me wearing her socks. I took them off. I kept my distance from the bag in the closet, but I talked about its contents with my friends.

Most people, when I told them about Sarah's abandoned laundry, were less interested in it than they were in other things, like movies and their own lives. A friend suggested I throw the clothes away—which would have been expedited by the fact that when I found them they were in a garbage bag. I wondered if Sarah had meant to throw them out but had forgotten to, in which case she would be upset to learn that I hadn't done it for her and was instead telling friends about her clothes, even if I omitted their more sultry details for decorum's sake.

When I told my friend Paul about the clothes at lunch, he asked why I hadn't washed them and said it was the first thing he would have done. I admitted, puzzled, that it hadn't occurred to me. At the time I couldn't figure out why not, but now, years later, I understand that Paul thought of this because he owned a house with a washer and dryer. I didn't have ready access to such appliances, so to wash Sarah's laundry would have meant a long walk to a laundromat and at least an hour devoted to cleaning things whose owner would never see them again.

When she departed Athens for Germany, Sarah may have forgotten altogether the castoffs in my closet that made up a fraction of the world's evidence of her passage through it. Having left America, she had other things—German things—to think about. Still, at night, alone, in Ohio, despite the Ohio things that worried me, I often lay awake with my mind fixed on the undone laundry.

❧ ❧ ❧

The apartment I rented was on the second floor of a building that stood on the slope of an Appalachian hill, on a street occupied mostly by college students. It consisted of a bedroom, a living room, a kitchenette, and a bathroom, all of which were ugly and old enough to have started disintegrating. The carpet was torn under the doorframes, the ceiling panels water-stained.

When I returned from my summer away, even before I saw the bag of laundry, it was clear that Sarah had left an impression on my home and that she knew more than I did about interior decorating. She had rearranged the living room to make more space for her, and me, to walk through. With a blanket she had covered the loveseat my brother had given me, which was stricken with permanent, multicolored stains left by his two sons. She had transformed the unsightly piece of upholstered furniture into something that was inoffensive—unless I lifted the blanket and peered underneath. In this way Sarah was a blessing, like Casper the Friendly Ghost.

From what I could tell, from the ways she had improved my home, and from the bottle I found in the bathroom that contained a substance that would stave off mold if I sprayed it into the shower after each use, Sarah was better at living in my home than I was. Most of the bottles I bought and emptied there contained Miller High Life, and they did nothing to prevent the onset of mold.

I had, on moving into it, named my apartment the Honeydew Melon. The name was a joke at first, something to enter as the first line of my address so that it appeared on junk mail. But naming the place had an effect, like naming a dog; it made the space I lived in more familiar. It might have also been a form of mail fraud, but I soon discovered that the name served another purpose still. It provided me a way to claim the space I took up, with my body, sheets, and predominantly brown wardrobe, to make it feel like my own, though I merely rented it.

Sarah had made my home more handsome, and cleaner, but she had also made the Melon seem less mine than hers. When I returned to it, for a moment I didn't recognize the place. Sarah was like a squatter who, by inhabiting and improving an abandoned building, earns the right to live there and renders immaterial its previous owner.

◥ ◥ ◥

In the months I spent living with Sarah's laundry, I wondered if I, too, had ever abandoned things when moving out of previous apartments. I remembered soon after I first wondered this, that I most certainly had. When I departed the first apartment I ever lived in, my friends and I left a menagerie of insect corpses smeared on our walls. We had spent our two years there killing moths, spiders, and other such creatures when they entered our home. Rather than clean them we would label each one with the time and date of its murder. When we moved out, we removed the Post-it notes that served as markers but left the bugs, because we knew our landlord had no intention of returning our security deposit.

In the second apartment I ever inhabited, I got into an argument with my girlfriend, an angry drunk who was, on this particular night, drunk. Her temper erupted and she threw at me a copy of *Catch-22* after trying in vain to tear it in half. She snatched from my desk a glass full of water and lobbed it at the nearest wall. It broke, soaking the floor and littering it with tiny pieces of glass that remained at least as long as my lease kept me in residence, despite my repeated efforts to vacuum them up. I would catch sight of the tiny shards as they glittered at me stubbornly from the carpet, and I wonder if they do it still, for someone else's eyes.

For as long as I lived in the Honeydew Melon, pasted in odd, unlikely corners were stickers the size of quarters with faded images of flower arrangements. One was on the door to my living room, one on a windowpane, one on the ceiling. Yet another was upside-down on the wall inside my closet, placed so that someone would have to snoop around for traces of other people to find it. I hadn't put them up. They could have been there for a decade. I never removed them. They served as evidence that the Melon had accumulated remnants of strangers long before Sarah, or I, came and went.

I considered it inevitable that when I moved I would leave something in the Melon by mistake—a paper clip, breadcrumbs, or dead skin and discarded eyelashes. My landlord had made no apparent effort to clean the apartment before I moved in and must have neglected to do it when I left. The

Melon, dutiful as always, would take possession of what remained—the next resident's inheritance—as soon as I was gone. It had done as much for Sarah, and for the legion of strangers who had lived between its walls, eating, sleeping, and being kept up at night by the neighbors.

❧ ❧ ❧

My neighbors were by far the loudest people I had ever been kept awake by. One night per week, the man across the hall would stay up late, drinking with his friends and playing video games. On one inspired night, he and they chanted, stomped against the floor, and pounded the walls, one of them giving off a prolonged shriek every few minutes until 5:00 in the morning. It sounded like they were having a violent, celebratory orgy.

The apartment above mine was inhabited by a rotation of loud people. The first was a man who would play, through his stereo, hours of bass-heavy music at high volume, all night. He accosted me one morning on my way out of the building to ask if I had called the police to report a noise violation. Someone had done this, he said, his eyes burning. It had been me, but when I lied and denied the charge, he proceeded to tell me a story: he used to live in the country and kept many dogs in his yard, but one day he enraged a man who later came to his yard and shot to death all but one of his dogs.

Eventually, he was replaced by a young college student, a woman with an unfortunate boyfriend. One night they fought and she threw him out, howling and slamming the door, demanding that he never return. Later that night he returned, scratching at her door, which was adjacent to mine. As he cooed to her, begging to be let in, she sat on the other side of her door and wept. I sat at my desk, listening with my head in my hands and wondered how many bad scenes the walls would contain before they finally came to pieces.

❧ ❧ ❧

When summer returned, I had to move away, and Sarah's clothes had to be reckoned with. Taking them with me would have meant claiming them as my property, but I didn't want to encumber myself with things I should never have had in the first place, so I made an active effort to dispose of the heavy garbage bag. I showed it to my friend Melanie and asked if she wanted anything in it. She remarked that she clearly didn't share Sarah's figure. She tried on the skirt, but it didn't fit, and then carried off a shirt anyway.

I didn't mention it, but when Melanie took the shirt I regretted ever bringing the clothes to her attention. It felt like she had taken something of mine.

Soon, Melanie found a woman in need of a skirt. As soon as we were introduced, this woman asked if she could have Sarah's. This skirtless woman was, like Sarah, a visiting student from Leipzig, and I saw that to hand the skirt over would have meant sending it on a trajectory back in Sarah's direction, but instead I told her I didn't have the skirt anymore. I told her I had already given the clothes away.

The day my lease ended, I was glad to leave the Melon. The woman upstairs had procured a little dog. When she wasn't home, which was most of the time, it pressed its nose against the screen of her open window and barked at nothing in particular. I could hear it for hours at a time, every single day.

The last thing I removed from the Melon was Sarah's dirty laundry. Nine months after her return to Germany, I rummaged through the sack she'd left and tossed her underwear into my last trash bag, as I thought she might have liked me to have done long before. The rest I carried to a Salvation Army donation bin half a mile away.

More than I cared what became of my Fiestaware, more than I cared about the Melon itself, with its ancient carpet and walls I had painted green, I cared about Sarah's bag of dirty laundry. I worried what might happen to the clothes when they left my custody. I knew, as I walked the bag down to the Salvation Army's roadside metal box, that I was letting go of something important. In an apartment full of objects—kitchen table, hand blender, dull chef's knife, unused knife sharpener, lamp—Sarah's sack of clothing was a thing—or thing filled with things—that seemed to mean something.

Standing before the donation bin, I thought I might actually miss it, this sack of someone else's stuff that had occupied my idle thoughts for nearly a year. I felt as though by having shared the Honeydew Melon, by having been so close for so much of the time, it and I had bonded. I pushed the metal door open and dropped the bag inside. As far as I know, I never saw its contents again.

Middens

K ATHRYN W INOGRAD

The packrat moved in last summer after the monsoons we had all prayed for failed. It was a summer of fire. The Teller County arsonist had already lit 13 quarter-acre fires in three days, and a meteor—"balls of fire," reported the astounded witnesses as far as New Mexico—grounded the air tankers over the Springer fire in late June. Then flames towered 200 feet up over Waldo Canyon, the air singed orange for days above the ashes, and the human remains eventually found in Mountain Shadow.

It was then I first saw the pinecones and the leaf litter ringing the porch board knothole directly beneath the old rocking chair in which I once nursed my daughters. Scanty, but a precise halo. I remember looking up as if the wind could be a god, stepping out of a paleo-sky to arrange this perfection of detritus like some Tibetan monk sand-painting the "world in harmony." But the world in flames, I swept the porch bare.

❧ ❧ ❧

In 1975, two years before I graduated from a small town high school where football rivals dubbed us "River Rats," *Newsweek* heralded "ominous signs that the Earth's weather patterns [had] begun to change dramatically." Concerned scientists pointed to declining growing seasons, rising equatorial temperatures, increased Northern Hemisphere snow cover, "the most devastating outbreak of tornadoes ever recorded," and a significant change in the amount of sunlight that hit the earth. The apparently cooling earth. Since 1940, the world temperature had in fact cooled, the "average ground temperatures in the Northern Hemisphere," the National Oceanic and Atmospheric Administration (NOAA) reported, "by half a degree."

"Melt the Arctic ice cap," the Chicken Littles of the time advised. "Cover it with black soot."

My mother remembers the deep Ohio freeze that year. My father, a general practitioner, drove down our gravel lane alongside the county cemetery each morning to his city office before winter broke open that first frozen tip of light. I think of him checking the breath and pulse of countless patients he might have healed, or not, while my mother worked our farm alone. That winter, she sledgehammered apart the milky rills of ice in the water troughs that thickened by morning, and then again by evening, despite the water heaters we floated.

"That year," she says, "25 degrees below zero. Days, I think."

What I remember is my sister and brother and me maneuvering the unwieldy blocks of ice from the troughs, the freezing water burning through our mittens, the steamy breath of Angus cows blurring the frozen world. And then, evenings, before the aluminum farm gates lit up with my father's returning headlights, we walked into the dark to pull the ice again, my father, pale in the dashboard light, driving blindly past us out of a precarious world we didn't quite know yet, but for the stones placed over the cold hearts of our neighboring dead.

Headlines or not, this was what we lived.

❱ ❱ ❱

Thirty-seven years later, my mother frail—"She's turned a corner," my brother warns me—my daughters, whom we once ferried newly born through the new snow, grown and gone, and my father, not that frozen world of my childhood, dead, the headlines repeat themselves, but with a twist. Yes, changing weather patterns, rising surface temperatures, "Frankenstorms," and "historic tornado outbreaks," but spawned, it seems, not by a cooling Earth this time, but a warming one, this world rife with open Arctic water, loss of summer sea ice, and the Greenland's Petermann Glacier calving for the second time in three years a 46-square-mile chunk of ice, two times the city of Manhattan, while fires in the west burn and we grieve what's lost. And what's soon to be lost.

"Global warming," my husband Leonard and the news say, "accelerated by human activity," even as scientists report the ending of an 11-year solar cycle, the most active in 8,000 years, the sun increasing its spew of flares and spots, solar radiation that the NOAA says "drives the weather machine" and what Mayan occultists say foretell the "killer" solar flares of cosmic align-ment, prophesized some 5,000 years ago to ignite this world into destruction, or renewal just two days ago.

I don't know what to believe.

My mother, visiting from an Ohio retirement home, clasps my elbow each time we walk outside, ice or sun. I ask her, as if she were my blind and shrinking Tiresias, what she thinks.

"I really don't know what to think. Or to do," she says, and I carefully hold her arm, so thin now, closer to me.

❧ ❧ ❧

Midden is a Middle English word that comes from an old Norse word, a combination of *dung* and *manure pile*. Think refuse, kitchen sink, paleologi-cal trash heap. An ancient domestic pile of bones, shells, whatever an ancient people used, and coprolites that archeologists study to know a dead people.

Or a packrat.

Or a world.

I think of Leonard and his Internet compatriots intent in their basements learning the most recent stats for global warming—"98 percent of scientists believe in it," Leonard tells me—how they would scoff at my apparently ignorant willfulness, worrying as I do over global warming and the predic-tions of every spokesperson, scientist or not, who tells me how my world will burn and end, or freeze and end. Yet there is that ice age of my childhood, and my half-memories of illustrated texts implicating cold-blooded, tail-brained dinosaurs in some kind of non-maternal expulsion, their young chipping themselves free from eggs untended, deserted, this the first of a whole litany of bitter disillusionments—my father dead, my mother going blind—I cannot get over.

Samuel Arbesman, a scholar at Kauffman Foundation and an expert in scientometrics, the "science of measuring the 'quality' of science," claims that just as there is a half-life to a radioactive isotope, there is a half-life to knowledge, the bulwark of "facts" we frail humans hunker against in the chaos of the unknown.

What is that half-life?

Forty-five years, unless, as I want to point out to Leonard, it is a fact published in a taxpayer-funded Louisiana school biology textbook proclaiming dinosaurs sunned themselves alongside Noah on the gopher wood of the Ark.

So I don't know what to believe.

Or I don't want to believe, the way I don't want to believe that a cabin built in the midst of an aspen grove could cause a kill-off of whole colonies, or disrupt the migration patterns of elk herds that more and more rarely graze in view of our windows. Or that in December, in the midst of what the news calls "this historic drought," after feet of snow and subzero temperatures, last summer's Fern Lake mountain fire—its genesis human—still smolders in remote pitchy loam unburned for 800 years.

◤ ◤ ◤

All night, after I swept the porch bare that first time, the dogs slept restless beneath the cracked window, the summer air heavy with its soot. The next morning, the little god-collage had returned, this time spreading to the other rocking chair, knuckles of pinecone and bark poised around a second knothole. And this time, little brown pellets clustered on my welcome mat.

Packrat or Woodrat, the field guide read, *classification in the rodent genus.*

White-throated or white-toothed, dusky-footed or big-eared, bushy-tailed or not, a rat. Despite its koala bear visage and its penchant for shiny foil and lost keys.

"A rat," my mother repeated over the phone last summer. "A big rat." And, then, not surprisingly, given her farm girl upbringing, she added, "Just shoot it," and laughed.

◤ ◤ ◤

Environmental interloper. Destroyer of aspen trees and middens my packrat resurrects each morning for my persistent sweepings. Self-professed global warming cynic, despite the fires that still burn in the valleys, singeing our sun red. I don't know what to do.

Dave, our mountain man rancher and professed killer of wildcats— "Seven or eight," he tells me, "shot right out of the trees"—visits on a Caterpillar with tires sized for lunar landscapes, and shakes his head when I show him the packrat signs. He pulls a long-nosed revolver from the cab toolbox, a gun I faintly remember from a collection of a past boyfriend, son of a sheriff deputy who each winter night, when the plows towered snow over the Iowa streets, no global warming there, tucked his weighty magnum beneath our bed sheets against what, I don't know. Dave warns me of engine block stowaways, incised carburetor wires.

"Mess with my truck and I will hunt you down," he warns my hidden packrat.

Leonard and I visit the neighbors near Eight Mile Creek, waterless now for the first time anyone can remember in this high plains ranching land dissected into 40 and 50 fenced acres. "Responsible hunters," our neighbors describe themselves. They follow the Forest Service guidelines for bow and rifle hunting, kill only what they are allowed, skin, then butcher the carcasses for their own consumption. The heads of their elk and deer hang from their walls, the largest clad in Santa Claus hats.

"Oh," they lament in unison, describe the packrat that homesteaded beneath their gas grill, the mysterious pounds of pinto beans she towed in each night and they threw out each morning. Even the hunters do not want to kill the packrat—"so cute, really,"—and describe a complex arrangement of bungee cords and the elevation of the gas grill that finally sent the packrat packing.

I buy a live animal trap at the Ace hardware in Cripple Creek. Little known packrat fact: packrat middens can grow up to five feet high and last for 50,000 years, cemented together by what's called "amberat," the viscous urine of the packrat. In western Utah, scientists found in one midden the still preserved bone of a camel extinct on this continent 12,500 years ago. That pile of pinecones, that halo as I called it beneath our rocking chairs? A packrat midden, evidenced by the tiny gold droplets I've lately noticed crystallized on our windowsill.

Leonard holds out a vanilla wafer. "Everyone likes vanilla wafers," he says, and carefully reaches into the metal cage to load the trigger spring. All night I worry: an accidental broken neck, the packrat exposed to the elements in this metal cage and frozen, despite Leonard's warnings of global warming. My daughter over the phone confirms this likely outcome, describing the hypothermic death of voles in the metal traps she helped place overnight in the high summer mountains during her week of scientific study. The next morning, the trap is sprung, and, of course, empty, our pristine wafer debauched by a nibble.

Meanwhile, the packrat's midden expands in piles along the cracks of the porch boards, deepens beneath the rocking chairs.

◣ ◣ ◣

Across the nation, in what was called the hottest summer in history, nine million acres burned, a record set only three times before. Down in the valleys, Colorado held funerals for the six dead and burned, this fire season called by our governor "the worst in history." January, and the red flag warnings continue. Already we fear the coming summer and its probable drought.

I remember after 9/11 how the Tibetan monks constructed a mandala, a sand painting at the Smithsonian museum, a rite of healing, they said. Then they destroyed it, a reminder of the world's and our impermanence. At its simplest, a mandala, like my porch halo, is a circle, organic or inorganic, "a cosmic diagram," I read, "that reminds us of our relation to the infinite, the world that extends both beyond and within our bodies and minds."

Once my mother and I passed hordes of Canadian geese amassed in a great circle where winter ice melted from a lake. My mother remembered the first time we saw Canadian geese flying over our farm, their high blaring calls sending her running, bird guide in hand, to the dam of the lake to watch the steady oars of their wings dip over the fields, until finally they were only a small echo in our ears. I remembered my father, still alive one early autumn morning when I did not know yet he would so early die in less than three months, his brain wasted by "plagues" and "tangles." He sat on a wooden bench my mother bought from Home Depot and set in their new backyard by a bulldozed lake so he could remember the farm she had sold to be nearer to my brother—the bench I took after my father died and keep now above the circle of aspens near our cabin. A keepsake of that day the geese blurred the air around him, my father already a stillness I could not touch in the world's flurry.

There are two kinds of fossils. Body fossils are the actual parts of the body left behind by the dead—their hair or their scales, their bones, their little chips of enamel. Trace fossils are the small tracks we leave behind in the earth, the places we have called our own: the dams of lakes, a 15-yard creek of flat stones and clay between the fence lines of a farm we may have once loved, or the woven bird nest we leave on top of a pair of cow horns to grace a barnyard where we once stood in the cold dark, our fathers already driving past us and our mothers waiting. It is said that *one single animal can make thousands and thousands of traces in its lifetime, but it will only leave behind one body when it dies.*

"Have you gotten rid of it yet?" my mother asks me over the phone. She is concerned about disease, about the viscous urine that I've told her scientists study from ancient middens for its record of rainwaters and the isotopes of cosmic particles that fall down upon us from whole solar systems, whole eternities we do not yet know.

Along the cabin's deck, beautiful circular patterns of pine needles appear.

Wind? Packrat? I do not touch them.

❧ ❧ ❧

Today, I am wondering about the exactitude of science—the science of climate change, to be precise. "We're toast," James Hansen proclaimed, NASA scientist who first sounded the global warming alarm back in 1988, choosing a record seven-day period of 100-plus degree temperatures in Washington, D.C. to fortuitously present decades of scientific findings to a sweating Congress and a wondering public. The concept of global warming went global, despite scientists' own disclaimer: "Weather is not climate. It's disingenuous to link the two."

Now the NOAA's 2012 Arctic Report Card records the lowest "sea ice extent" since satellite observation began in 1979 and record-breaking "near-ice sheet-wide surface melting" in Greenland; both conditions NOAA points to as indicators of the continued real impact of 30 years of global warming. Yet, in Antarctica, there is a significant increase of sea ice, and the "snow extent" in the Northern Hemisphere has been at record highs. And this past January, Arctic ice increased at a "slightly higher average for the month," according to the National Snow and Ice Data Center, a fact I'll cling to.

Paleoclimatologists, the scientists who study past climates, study climate change through what they call "proxy," a word I look up, which means "the authority or power to act for another." They study the trace fossils of the earth, the hardened midden where extinct grass pollen once blew into it with the wind, the rings of trees to mark the rains that bring growth, the growth bands of coral, the bore holes and the ice cores they drill for ancient signs of heat and cold, so few the ways to know the world that existed before us, except in the little signs it gives us, its substitutions.

A study of southwestern ponderosa pine and tree rings to determine the connection between sustained drought and the "mega fires" of the past years reveal that 1,500 years ago the droughts of the Medieval Warm Period were more severe but the fires less so because of the continual surface burning that went on and saved the mature trees from the devastation of crown fire, an "understory burning" in modern times that we have suppressed. In a Colorado cave, a packrat midden reveals the bones and teeth of ancestral voles a million years old that packrats once killed, leaving an evidence of an evolving species of voles that suggests a whole flux of climate change, glacial and warming, because of the earth's spin or its axis or the shape of its orbit. We think.

I think of my daughter and her classmates in this last summer of fire, when men and women died in their cars, in their own homes, disbelieving the encroaching flames, when lightning struck Flagstaff Mountain, burning toward Upper Skunk Canyon and I feared for my daughter, how she and her classmates dipped small mammals into fluorescent powder and released them to the chaotic dark, their frenetic orbits shining through the tinder grass.

"Somebody should shake the geese eggs," my mother says. I look at her. "In the dark, so the neighbors can't see. Just give them a little shake." She laughs and I am glad to see it, her sadness the trace fossil I fear I'll carry with me. Later, when Leonard and I drive past the lakeside geese, an influx of migration, I have been told, because of global warming, I tell him what my mother says, "Just shake the eggs."

A minute of silence, Leonard thinking, and then, bird lover, global warming prophet, love, he pulls his hands from the steering wheel, slaps them over his face." Oh, god! oh god!"

❧ ❧ ❧

The Tibetan monks say that to have a mandala there must be one to view it, a "you" to enter the "beauty of perfection" that is the Buddha's mind.

I no longer sweep the porch bare. Instead, Leonard and I leave out apple cores and wilted dinner salad, strewing it all over the snow-stiffened cinquefoil I transplanted alongside the cabin porch in shovelfuls last fall, my mouth bitter with ash and smoke that finally the spare winter snows have quelled. I won't tell my mother this when I walk out with her again, arm in arm, into this prophetic world of ice and fire that already she grieves, change the only impending certainty we know. What will it finally matter, I ask myself, that we fed a packrat that set up housekeeping beneath our porch? Or that we didn't catch it? Or didn't shoot it? As if my mother really would.

On occasion, and only in the most forgiving, anonymous dark, Leonard and I leave crumpled slips of Reynolds Wrap on the blue bird welcome mat like a constellation of origami stars that all night we dream in circles. Our windows still closed for winter, our nocturnal packrat wends its way around and around the stone walls of our cabin, our proxy, as I see it now, a little god we can live with, piling our porch with its pinecones and needles while the first spring catkins of our aspen blow free, these traces preserved.

The Avocado

JILL CHRISTMAN

f the answer was the smooth, brown pit at the center of a ripe avocado I bought for breakfast from the man on the corner in San Jose, Costa Rica, then the question began with the slippery green nubs on the surface, the ones I ran my thumb across for courage as I walked back to my single bed in the pension, past a group of men on the street, all of them hissing *que guapa que guapa que guapa*. Twenty years old, blue-eyed and dark-haired, I didn't know my own beauty, would never have thought to consider such a phrase—*my own beauty*—but I held a growing sense of my body's place at the center of things. I mean this in a geological way: the shifting and slipping of solids and liquids, the crunching of plates, the obliteration of the eruption, and, afterward, the layering, the building up.

At home in Oregon, before the tow truck hit my fiancé's van in the cold November of the previous year, I wore tight sweaters, white cowboy boots, and snug jeans with a thin ribbon of lace around my too-small waist. Before the accident made Colin's body something they wouldn't even let me see, never mind touch, I still counted catcalls from the yogurt shop to my Shakespeare class, but I had a dawning understanding that my heart's acceleration in the electric heat from strangers on the street was more fear than power, more fuck you than fun.

This tectonic shift may be credited partially to my first women's studies class, but the real change came from the way Colin loved me. Of course he loved my body, as I loved his, but he also loved *me*. I'd been having sex since my mid-teens and before that, when I was a child—a bedrock violation, my body the property of our neighbor across the field long before I knew it was mine. Before Colin, I'd held all that down, buried deep, not knowing how much work I had to do before my body was mine—bones and flesh, skin and hair, hard parts and soft parts—a body I could share if I wanted, without giving anything away.

It makes sense, then, that the teenage sex I had before Colin was like something I watched on TV—not all bad, sometimes comical, never better than a book, but always from a distance, always from the other side of a screen. Before Colin, I didn't stay in my body for sex. I slipped out, a curl of steam, a wisp of vapor, and no one seemed to notice she was gone. Not even me. But Colin loved me enough to know this and we practiced. He'd watch for my departure, and if something pulled me away, he would stop whatever he was doing and lie next to me holding my hand. Together we were safe and together we could burn.

In the single year we had together, Colin beckoned me down from the walls, back from the edges, to inhabit my body, a real woman's body. With his fingers, his tongue, the firm pressure of all of him, he walked the ledge of my collarbone, fed the curved lines of my ribs, and kissed—again and again—the freckled birthmark spreading across the top third of my left thigh. In the middle-school dressing room, the mean girls had pointed, calling out my *dirty spot*, heckling me to *wash off the mud*, but Colin saw something else. "Look," he said, turning my hip with his palm. "A lion. She's running, looking over her shoulder." And I could see her there. *Yes.* Together, we roared, and then Colin took his own body and went away. He saved my life, and then he died.

On the day of that perfect avocado, I was four months into a kind of volcanic winter, the sun occluded by the ash that rose up when Colin had burned, when his strong, golden, six-foot-two body—so beautiful—had become something the man in the side room at the funeral home could hand to me in a small cardboard box.

I remember being surprised by the weight, the muscles in my arms tightening to pull him to my chest, feeling the heat in the box when the ashes shifted. *No. No.*

Now what?

Sliding down the continent on a black wash of grief, I hid my diminished self in a shapeless dress, the line falling straight and loose from top to bottom, my skin untouched except the top of my well-covered breasts and my shins, tickled by the cotton hem with each stride, bright orange poppies on pale blue backing. I marched straight-lipped and eyes ahead through the path the men cleared, holding my avocado in both hands like a gift. I wondered if they could read my sad story in my eyes.

What if I stopped and told them? What if I handed one of them my avocado and he whipped a blade from his back pocket to carve the fruit into trembling green slices to share? What if I let him lay one on my tongue?

Still hissing, the men stepped back, parting the waters of their male bodies, and I moved through. Nobody touched me, not even a brush of my dress, and I didn't stop walking. I didn't even look. Too much color, I thought; orange poppies were a reckless choice for a grieving girl, but I kept moving, stroking the hide on my avocado, my own skin rippling like a horse shooing a fly with a tremor of flesh. *Que guapa sssssssssssssssss.* The men were not aggressive, or even unkind. They sent me around the corner to the heavy wooden door of my pension with more words I couldn't understand then and cannot remember now.

But I remember the way the loneliness of that narrow bed shifted when I palmed the avocado, my alligator pear, pressing my knife into the tough skin until the tip plunged through flesh, knocking against the pit as if against a door, and hearing no answer, just the communal shower through the thin wall, I pulled the blade around the equator until she fell open, divided, onto the clear plastic bag I'd laid out as a placemat.

The flesh inside was perfect, almost too beautiful to eat. Avocado green is not, in fact, the desexed color of 1970s stand mixers, but something more complicated, a gradation of shade from buttercream near the nut-brown pit to deep-shade-in-the-forest green at the perimeter where flesh meets frame. On one hemisphere, the clinging brown pit glowed gold, a cross-sectioned woman, heavy with child. On the other side, a hollow, a vacancy, the curvature where something vital had been but was now gone.

I ate that shadowed side first. After color, texture is all, and the merchant on the corner with his basket and I in my traveling dress had captured our fruit in that closing window when my plastic spoon slipped through the flesh to scoop morsels like ice cream not too long out of the freezer: yielding but firm, so deliciously transient.

Colin had been dead for one season—a single winter—and here was a succulent loneliness I could hold on my tongue, a sensuality I could take in.

Stay here, I ordered myself. *Don't go.*

The accident happened at a crossroads in Tillamook, a small town on the coast of Oregon most famous for cheddar cheese. How was I to know when I let Colin go that this tiny, wet city would be so prone to burning? What's notable about Tillamook historically is also the thing that brought Colin and his workmates, all young men, to the dark crossroads where they died that night: during World War II, the Navy built two of the world's largest free-standing wooden structures in Tillamook, hangars massive enough to play six games of football simultaneously—in each one. On that soggy day in November, Colin and his friends had been in one of those giant hangars preparing a Virgin lightship for the next day's planned inflation. The blimps were a pet project of British entrepreneur Richard Branson, extreme adventurer and would-be knight. I don't blame Branson for what happened to Colin, but whenever I hear about his high-risk attempts in balloons or speedboats or spaceships, I think: *Sir Richard, were the brakes good on that company van? Was your guy okay to drive? Did you leave some men behind on life's big adventure?*

Twenty-four years later, Colin has been dead longer than the twenty-two years he was alive, I am old enough to be mother to the young man he was when he died, and the scope of that perspective looks to me like a cavernous, wood-framed building, a wonder of engineering, and the last structure Colin ever stood in, a space big enough to fly a jet plane through. Three young men died that night, two British and one American—Colin—and a second American survived, diminished. I wonder now if they felt small in that looming, covered air, or whether the sense of sheer enormity—I remember Colin stretching his long arms, fingers up and open, as if he were trying to carry a cloud, trying to explain to me the size, the hugeness—made these young men feel bigger, more invincible, as they climbed into the minivan, not bothering with seatbelts, and headed down the road for a pizza.

It makes me sad now to think they died hungry.

In the days after the phone call came in, I couldn't eat and I couldn't stop vomiting. I maintain only flickers of memory from these first weeks, but I remember the ginger snaps. With Colin's sisters and brothers and parents all around me, numb or wailing or rocking in the lava flow of deep grief—of seven children, Colin had been the baby, their *baby*—I know I wasn't the only one who needed something I could swallow, but my recollection is that the ginger snaps were brought home especially for me. Why can't I remember any faces? Why can I better remember the yellow box of dry, round cookies than the decimated family who tried to feed me? The psychiatrist at my school had called in a prescription for suppositories to calm me down, stop the vomiting, and put me to sleep. But I wasn't using them faithfully. I wanted to be awake if Colin visited me in the night. I was a shattered body waiting for one that had been burned to dust. I wanted to follow him, but someone (my mother? Colin's mother? his sister?) broke off a piece of ginger snap and made me stick out my tongue. The fragment of wafer stuck there. I pulled in my tongue like a toad, hoping they could now let me die.

There are other parts of the story that seem to matter, although I'm not sure where they fit in, how to tell them. When we drove to Tillamook to pick up Colin's ashes, we stopped by the crossroads where he died and I thought, *This is the last place Colin was alive. I am standing where Colin took his last breath.* In the dirt, I found a fragment of mirror. I can't remember if we went to the crossroads on the day of the funeral home, or if they wouldn't let me then, if I drove back to Tillamook, later, alone. I know I went back. Now I can see the intersection of Highway 101 and Long Prairie Road on Google Maps. I can swoop down to street level and with a stroke of my finger, turn my gaze, surprised by the blow to the gut, startling myself by thinking, still, *This is the last place Colin was alive. I am standing where Colin took his last breath.*

In 1992, three years after the accident, there was a fire in Hangar A. Apparently, they'd been using the giant blimp structure to store hay, lots of hay—7,600 tons of dry tinder. Fifteen fire engines rushed to the scene and unable to enter the burning building, 70 firefighters stood in the dark, faces glowing, and watched one of the two largest free-span wooden structures in the world burn to the ground.

It must have been spectacular. A conflagration to beat all conflagrations.

We drove with Colin's ashes to the ranch in northern California where he'd played with his dogs and learned to catch calves. We made a mound of him on a hill, almost a sand castle. When the rest of the family stumbled back to the barn for the pancake breakfast, they let me stay with Colin on my knees, my mind frantic. What could I do? What now?

Here is what I did: I sprinkled some ashes into my palm, thick, grainy pieces of bone, and I kissed them. I licked him from my lips, felt him crunch between my teeth. I told him to stay with me. I explained my sudden plan, an inspiration: *I am taking you into me.*

Stay with me. Don't go.

In slow spoonfuls, on my bed in the pension, I ate only half of the avocado and wrapped the other in the plastic bag to save, knowing where the pit touched the flesh, the enzymes would preserve the green. I wasn't traveling alone in Costa Rica, but I usually *was* alone. My traveling companions were also grieving, and we had trouble finding each other in our separate fogs. Colin's brother, the one with the same olive skin and deep brown eyes but ten years older, was there for the same reason I was—to escape his grief, or walk through it and into the rainforest's center. His girlfriend was there, too, but on the day I'd flown in, they'd broken up, and she was grieving the loss of her own little brother, murdered. I came to realize their parallel pain was the one and only thing that could have brought these two opposing forces together even for a night. She despised me. She hated me for being young, making disgusted noises in her throat and tossing her dusty blond hair like a weapon when we passed the desk of the pension together and the young clerk watched me the way he always did, moist-eyed and trembling.

On the day of the avocado, I told the clerk at the desk—who had become my friend—about the men and their hissing. He smiled longingly and said in his perfect English: "No, no, señorita. They don't mean to scare you or insult you. They want to give you a compliment. They want to tell you that you are beautiful. That's all. Take their compliment and be happy. Be happy, señorita."

That afternoon we boarded a bus north to see Arenal, the always-smoking volcano. I know it takes at least three hours to get there from San Jose, but we traveled on so many buses for so many hours and it was so many years ago, I'm not confident I can pick this day out from all the others. I want to say there was rain that day and that we boarded a more modern bus with high-backed, individual, Greyhound-style seats for the first leg before getting dropped off during an afternoon storm in a little town where I drank an icy Orange Crush from a thick glass bottle, standing with my back against the wall while the heavy rain sluiced off the awning and splashed my sandaled toes. When the next bus finally came, it was bench-seated, like a school bus, and we bounced the rest of the way.

For once, there was no dust. The rain had wet down the road to the volcano. I felt for my avocado through the nylon on my waist pack to make sure it was not getting smashed. Everything that touched my body—the warm tin siding on my back, the smooth bottle on my lips, the hard seat against my thighs, my own reaching hand on my belly near the avocado—made me think of Colin.

No body to feel another day's touches. No body to touch my body. No body.

Half a lifetime ago, on the bus to Arenal, I couldn't yet know how this female body of mine would rise up in grief's heat, a collision of continental and oceanic plates, the solid I could touch, holding me together, and the liquid that was most of me, bubbling, carrying me along through another 20 years in my changing form from grieving girl to lover, lover, lover, then wife, then mother, my baby girl thriving, then grieving again—the new baby in my womb damaged, my body opened up to take him out, my body the site of our loss and grief, my body the scene of the accident, my whispered prayer to Colin: *Please take care of my baby. Keep him warm. Don't let him go hungry.*

After the surgery that removed our son from my womb, I wondered how my husband would ever touch me again without thinking about what we'd made together, imperfectly, and then lost, with that same crashing together of human imperfection. More loss, more bleeding, and then another birth, a living son to join our daughter, all of us waiting and wanting, and me lying in our huge bed, nursing my new baby boy, thinking: *How will I ever be grateful enough for my body and what she has done?*

When we finally arrived, I sat alone on a log by the lake with my avocado, savoring my last bites with sputtering Arenal rising up before me. She was like a volcano from a science fair, hand-shaped with clay by eager hands into a perfect cone. She was quintessential, the platonic ideal, all of us imperfect in her smoking shadow.

After so many disappointments, Arenal was the volcano I expected her to be.

Licking the buttery green from my spoon, I looked down and noticed an astounding line of leafcutter ants carrying bright, freshly cut leaves in their mandibles. Swaying past in the current of their own community, the shiny ants looked like catamarans with outsized sails. I'd missed the beginning of the line and would never see the end. I took pity and after scraping the avocado clean, I put the shell in the ants' path, hoping my clean would be their idea of a feast, an avocado cruise, but the ants diverted their line, like green water around a rock, and kept moving, unfazed and unwavering, eyes ahead.

I meant only to be kind, to offer the only thing I had to give.

Arenal is all woman. She's a composite volcano, which means that she's built herself up in layers of hardened lava and pumice and ash, explosion after explosion, holding her magma deep in her core until she can't any longer. Until she loses it. And then even her spewed rage and grief and sorrow harden, make her bigger.

Arenal rose up because of what the seismologists call convergence. In her case, an oceanic plate colliding with a continental plate, with no place to go but up.

In 1990, when I was there with my avocado, Arenal had been steaming and spewing daily since a summer afternoon in 1968 when, after four centuries of quiet dormancy, she blew, burning three villages and killing 87 villagers. Having come into her power, Arenal kept it up for 30 years, until a day in May 1998, when she erupted 23 times in a single afternoon and then gave up her daily venting.

In the seventeenth century, German astronomer Johannes Kepler believed volcanoes were ducts for the earth's tears. I had eaten the last of my avocado, the ants marched onward with their wavering loads, and Arenal and I sat together and wept.

In my palm, all I had left of my avocado was the impossibly smooth pit. Stroking the slippery seed with my thumb, I held the pit to my cheek, the answer to the question I'd been asking all day—walking past the men on the street, sitting alone in the narrow bed, sheltering from the downpour against the warm building, careening towards the volcano on the jolting bus, taking in my first view of Arenal, my first volcano, and the ants, always leaving. I touched my lips to the unbroken shell, remembering how my mom had once used toothpicks to suspend an avocado pit over water in a jar, how amazed we were by the roots bursting through the casing, fissuring the pit like an eruption, or an accident.

Breaking open, to begin again.

Our son's birth was difficult. Before I could go into labor naturally, I panicked, suddenly sure he would die if we didn't get him out, so I asked to be induced. If the midwife would puncture the amniotic sac and bring my baby's head down to knock on the cervical door, then I would finish the job. I would use my power to get him born, alive and breathing.

In the sixteenth hour, after the kind of pain that made me sure I would die, split open and die, the midwife told me it was time. She guided my hands down and touched them to my son's head—thick, wet hair and round, solid skull. I walked my fingers down to his ears. His ears!

"Now push and pull him up onto your chest," she instructed.

The doctor had arrived. He said, "Push past the burn. Feel the burn and push through it."

I felt the searing burn, on fire but not really a pain now, just flame. I clasped my baby's head, his ears tucked into my palms, and in a flood of my body's power, every kind of power, I pushed him out and guided his slippery body with my own hands up onto my waiting chest and our side of this crazy, hot, shifting, heartbreaking, beautiful world.

Peer Support

PAT RATHBONE

volunteer for an outfit called PCAN, Pancreatic Cancer Action Network. You don't want what it takes to do my job. But I am a psychotherapist, as well as a person who has— has had?—pancreatic cancer, so I thought my skills would make me a good candidate to help others. Newly diagnosed patients can phone someone experienced. I had about a year's experience when I signed on. Too much; not enough.

Betsy, a woman my age, calls. She has recently been released from the hospital after a Whipple. The Whipple is the Mt. Everest of surgery—ask a doc who has done one. Betsy is a therapist too. Her diagnosis is the same as mine, except they found a positive lymph node outside her pancreas. "Just one," she says.

She is alone, never married, recently moved from the Bay Area to a planned community near San Luis. I couldn't imagine going through the months ahead without a partner. Who will call the visiting nurse when the electric drain attached to her incision screams, scaring the dog, and fails to pump? Who will change her dressings, drive her to chemo, cook the weird foods she craves?

Like me, she is furious that the life she planned is lost. "I don't want this marvelous new life survivors tout. I want the old one where I didn't have to appreciate every day!" But she is resourceful: before she called me, she tracked down a program that provides nutritional counseling and a group that will pay for a consult when she is well enough to travel. She found a program that would pay her airfare, too. I tell her about the vaccine trial I hope to join. I contacted them first when I was still in chemo, traveled to Baltimore, was assured of acceptance into the next cohort.

She is upbeat. I'm supposed to support *her*, I think. The next day I call Baltimore—soon, they say.

After talking to Betsy, I call Baltimore every few weeks. My oncologist, Rebecca, calls too. The physician who runs the study is impressed by that; he sends her warm emails. He says no oncologist has ever supported a patient for his trial. I think he'd like to know her better.

At last he emails that the next phase of the trial is about to begin and I should contact the study nurse to book an appointment. The next day he emails again, rescinding the invitation. I have lived too long since surgery and no longer qualify for his vaccine. Eighteen months is their limit. "Sorry," he says.

I give Betsy his name and, having barely finished her initial treatment, she is accepted at once. She is grateful. We agree that she is taking my place.

◣ ◣ ◣

Other voices I hear on the phone haunt me. They are frightened voices, not upbeat at all. A man is living alone somewhere in Boston—he could be down my street. I don't understand his story. Why was it a "chest doctor" who told Joe he had pancreatic cancer? Why has no physician seen him since that distressing news six weeks ago?

Mostly he wants reassurance that he can "beat this," so the story dribbles out around the edge of his desperation. The Ride took him to an appointment with an oncologist, but though he waited hours, no one saw him. The Ride transports disabled people. Another dribble of information: he is on oxygen. And he has diabetes. He asks me questions: what did *I* do? I had surgery. No one has suggested surgery to him. Well no, I think. You don't have a physician to recommend any treatment. "How long ago did you have surgery?" he asks. Now it is over two years. I don't want to remember, but the memory seems like a film.

Joe is crying. "Pat," he says. "I have to beat this."

Really, over and over, this is what he says.

Rudely I interrupt: "How old are you?" I don't know where that came from, but he answers—he is 86.

Wow. Sometimes I dream of 80. My mother told me 80 was okay, 85 too old, but at 90 she seemed still to enjoy herself, driving her younger friends around, playing bridge.

I ask how much longer he wants to live. This seems a terrible question, but it slows the rush of his words. I can hear him think. I have rearranged aspects of his experience. I know then that he has been feeling very young, a robust Irish man in his prime, his future, his last decades stolen. Now he will never meet the woman who will fix him a good meal, drive him about in *her* car.

"A couple of years," he says after a long pause—during which he aged 30 years. "Seems a reasonable hope," I say. But to get anywhere close, he'd need excellent care.

Two weeks later he tells me he has an appointment. But why is it an appointment with a thoracic oncologist? What's with his chest? I know by his silence that he wants me to go with him, but he won't ask. I've fallen for him. He reminds me of another Irish man, who painted my house years ago in Jamaica Plain. "Pat," Martin would whine, my short name a keening four measures, "make me a sandwich?" I see the next two months, and I don't volunteer. Instead I help him write a list of questions he must ask the doctor.

He doesn't call me after the appointment. Though I don't usually do this, I call him. The phone rings and rings, but no one answers. I call for weeks, almost every day, as he used to call me, but still there is no answer.

◣ ◣ ◣

A man named Bob phones from a southern resort town. He is more with it than Joe, less anxious, but even more depressed. He has had six weeks of chemo and played golf each day. They are trying to shrink his tumor so that eventually they might attempt surgery. The chemo has not been successful. No more gemcitabine, he will move to the stronger stuff. I shudder, having talked to others on this regimen. Then radiation. Unless, I think, he quits before that.

Bob says he can't get off the couch. Over and over he repeats, "I can't eat, can't play golf, can't get off the couch." He won't go to lunch with his golf buddies; he won't even play nine holes. (I know this is serious. I'm a golfer.) His kids up north tell him he has to talk to someone, so he calls PCAN and gets my name. By talk to someone, they mean therapy, of course. He's a New Yorker, they are New Yorkers: you can't get off the couch, you call a shrink. Well, I am that too, I tell him.

He says again, "I played golf every day they gave me chemo." Chemo in the morning, golf in the afternoon. Or maybe it was the other way around—that would make more sense to me.

I talk to him about golf. About the new battery-operated trolley I bought because I no longer have the energy to push the Sun Mountain Speedcart, how I gave up carrying five years ago, even before pancreatic cancer, so I can't blame everything on that. He rides, but then he has some problem with his legs.

He *used* to ride—now he won't do anything. He is starving, down to 140 pounds. I remember my father under 100 pounds, his skin like fine tissue paper wrapping the wires of his body. But that was the disease, not depression.

"How come? You blast through chemo and now you go limp?"

She left after the chemo. Bob understands because she has "buried a husband." Because he understands, it doesn't matter. She drove him to chemo every day and she just couldn't go on. He understands. She "buried a husband."

I understand her too. Once I could not untangle myself from a lover facing a dire diagnosis: a bad biopsy would mean the loss of half her pelvis and a leg. Terrified, I knew I would never be able to leave if this happened. A week after surgery, she called from the hospital, woke me at midnight with the news: benign. I can live with what I did that night.

But I am talking to Bob, who is on his couch. "She left you. She couldn't go through it again, fine—but she left you alone."

"I retired too early," he says. In the following pause, he is listening to all the voices who urged him to keep working. His kids, his friends up north, the fellows at the shop. What, you crazy? No one plays golf all day! People down there, they're different. It's the south for fuck's sake! And he'd shown them. Met a woman. Started a relationship. And those guys still knocking around their single, divorced, empty lives.

"Well," he says after an hour or so. "Thank you. My kids said I should talk to a psychologist, and I guess I have."

❮ ❮ ❮

Betsy has three infusions of the vaccine, each a month apart, and then a recurrence of cancer. "I'm lucky it's not in a major organ," she says. "But I've flunked out of our trial."

We both know this means more chemo. More chemo is always worse chemo. She thinks this new, stronger chemo combo—three in one—will cure her cancer.

Betsy emails frequently in the next months. The side effects of the chemo are as grim as I imagined. "As soon as the fungus on my tongue clears up so I can talk, I'll call," she writes. She tries new supplements and acupuncture for her intense fatigue. She organizes a patient blog, talking to folks who throw scary acronyms around, abbreviations for new forms of torture. Somehow she is still upbeat.

One day I get an email, I'VE GOT TO TELL YOU in the subject line. Attached is a picture of a short, pretty woman and a man. His arm is draped around her shoulder. He is tall, white-haired, nice looking; three dogs are at their feet.

Betsy is very happy, but one day she calls in tears. "I just had a melt-down," she says. At the last infusion, her oncologist said if she can just get through this series, which has damn near killed her, maybe she can get a break from treatment. "A break?" What does he *mean*? she wants to know. She knows. I know.

◥ ◥ ◥

Jill is different. For one thing, she is younger than Betsy or Bob or Joe or the rest of the people who call, and her energy amazes me. "I had a Whipple," she begins, "and the problem is the scar."

This is familiar ground. I have a great deal of pain at the wound site.

"So what do I tell guys?" she asks. Her mother told her not to say she had cancer, but how should she explain the scar? "Not that I sleep with them on the first date," she adds.

Before I can respond, she fills me in on her diagnosis (a very good one, as diagnoses go) and the treatment recommended by a consulting oncologist in Boston. I don't tell her I have seen him too.

"My doctor here in Pennsylvania told me the odds of a cure are 95 percent." Yes, that's what I'd heard, too—for her disease. "Which really means a sure thing, right? Some of those guys die of heart attacks." She talks very fast. I hardly have time to think.

I tell her she is lucky. She tells me they shouldn't lump her disease with pancreatic cancer. Then why call me?

"But that Dr. K in Boston, he said no, it's aggressive, 60 percent. I told him about the 95 percent, but he says if I do everything he says, which is a lot more than the other doc recommended, 60 percent."

She can't believe they disagree. Who is right? she wants to know. Who will tell her the truth? Do I know? If not, who should she see next? Should she go to Johns Hopkins?

"It's a number," I say.

"But an important number."

"What difference does it make?"

"What difference?" If I were in the room, she would throw the phone at me.

"If you're cured, who is right?" I ask. "Was it because you're in the 60 percent or the 95 percent?" I don't mention the other possibility. I don't say, "Who will you sue if you die?"

◥ ◥ ◥

Betsy has only two more hideous treatments. She can't feel her fingers or her toes and it is a struggle to walk around the block. She wants me to be the first to know: she and Lyman will marry in eight weeks, two weeks after she's done. Just his children, her nephew, a few close friends. Her condo is on the market—they were living in his anyway. What do I think about a lavender dress? She hasn't been able to find one and is thinking of having it made. But the cost! "And no presents," she says. "Absolutely no presents. Make a donation to PCAN, instead."

I have given. I tithe. I barter, too: I give up sleep for them and receive bad dreams in return. I try not to take calls in the evening, but yesterday a new patient phoned late, a woman who had a recurrence after three disease-free years. It has been three years for me. I thought three years was an almost guarantee. Last night I dreamed I was about to leave our local hospital, just about to step into the round, revolving door to the outside world. My doctor, white coated, stopped me: "I'm going to admit you," he said.

"But why?" I heard my own ragged voice.

He turned to leave on his important rounds, but glanced back over his shoulder. "Because I can."

He can claim Betsy, too. But before he does, I will gather a riot of blue and purple flowers to match her dress: scilla, hyacinth, iris, lavender, delphinium, and veronica. Moving south from Massachusetts, I will tear them from the earth as they bloom in milder states. Then I will carry them west, across the land.

Within this Kingdom

AMANDA GIRACCA

1.

ast summer I repotted several cymbidium orchids. "Orchid" likely conjures up the loveliest of flowers, something too delicate to mess with, but the cymbidiums needed a firm hand. Over time they had migrated to the edge of their pots, as though trying to glacially ooze their way out and back to the wild. A ring of healthy lance-like leaves stood sentinel at the edge of the terracotta, and in the center was a mass of bloomed-out remnants, a cluster of moldering knobs in various forms of decay. Some of the knobs, when I picked away at them, revealed the subtlest hint of white material—promise that they might sprout again. I turned each pot on its side, tucked it between my knees, and pulled until the mass of roots slid out along with the fir bark chips they'd been nestled in. I laid the plant across the greenhouse floor, took a small pruning saw and made an incision down the center of the plant, stuck my fingers in and pried it open. Then I made smaller incisions with the saw, grinding away the decayed material, and when the cuts became too small for the saw, I took a pair of pruners and snipped until I was left with just a small pile of fresh, promising shoots.

If all went well, by winter, the larger sprouts would shoot out racemes loaded with butter-colored flowers. The inner petals would have magenta freckles, and a central petal—a labellum—would protrude tongue-like, almost rudely, with a small hood cupped over the top. Two yellow pollen bumps rest on top of the labellum, ridged just the right way to capture pollen off the legs of an insect going in. Cymbidiums flower for weeks on end, each plant having maybe five to ten racemes, each raceme over a foot tall and holding dozens of the mesmerizingly asymmetrical blossoms.

Cymbidium comes from the Greek *kumbe*, cup, the flowers being filled with the slightest drop of nectar that keeps bees nuzzling after it, like drunkards after dregs of mead. "The King of Fragrance," Confucius is said to have called them, although he may have meant they emit their fragrance *for* kings. The cymbidiums I have known are scentless. Our minds are quick to compare the flowers with female genitalia—yet "orchid" comes from the Greek *órkhis*, meaning testicle, because of the shape of the pseudobulbs, "pseudo" because this bulb doesn't actually go underground, but lodges itself on surfaces above ground and functions more like a stem, the leaves of the orchid growing directly out of it.

I've often wondered what it would be like to stumble upon a bunch of flowering cymbidiums in the wild, the way the naturalist Alexander von Humboldt saw them as he traveled through the tropical regions of South America at the turn of the nineteenth century. He observed them at a roaring cataract on his way to the Orinoco River, where the plunging torrents cast the area in a "perpetual verdure." More than the flower, it's the experience I've craved—to *discover* such beauty. Not to be the one here, trapped with such rote duties, but to be out in the world. The epiphytic orchids von Humboldt found grew up the trunks of giant fig trees along with begonias, vines, and vanilla orchids. A single trunk along the Atures Rapids on the Orinico, von Humboldt said, had more plants than an extensive plot of land in Europe.

Often, staring at my greenhouse cymbidiums, I've tried to locate the tropical mountainside, the perpetual verdure, within the plant, to understand how people succeeded in domesticating all these pieces from so many remote corners of the world. I look for the setting, the home of the orchids—or rather, of these greenhouse orchids' distant ancestors—that they left behind when they were uprooted and tucked into a naturalist's satchel. I envision a piece of root, a pseudobulb, kept moist enough not to dry out, dry enough not to mold, cared for and brought back to Europe, coaxed back to life in a greenhouse. I consider the centuries of orchids being split and sawed and redistributed, orchids traveling over the ocean from one hemisphere to another. That story fascinates me—and also disturbs me. How did these orchids end up *here*, in a private greenhouse in western Massachusetts? It's the source I want to locate—a rocky hillside in the Himalayas with cymbidiums spilling over a ledge, the mossy bank alongside a cascading waterfall in South America.

The greenhouse I worked in had both orchids and a fig tree, but they did not grow together—each was quarantined to its own separate pot in a separate portion of the greenhouse—orchids on steel shelves near the entrance, the fig tucked in a back corner. When I finished repotting, my orchids didn't look particularly happy; they tilted awkwardly, rootless now in the fresh fir bark chips.

"They'll catch," said my boss, Jenna, the following week when we assessed my repotting efforts. "Of course they're not going to look happy at first. But you did it right." Then she did what she always does, stuck her fingers down into the pot, scooping some orchid medium into a little pile so she could thrust her hand down deep. "It's easy to overwater them at this stage," she said, pulling up a handful of saturated fir bark chips from the bottom of the pot. "So go light for awhile."

The glass greenhouse we worked in belonged to an early twentieth-century mansion. The property also had a caretaker's cottage, an old carriage house, and several barns, all of which had been sitting vacant for two years as the new owners slowly refurbished the house. They sent their plants first, perhaps unsure of how long their transition would take, and for two years we attended the plants even though no one lived there. The greenhouse held a dozen other species of orchids, along with cacti, lemon trees, banana trees, passionflowers, Boston ferns, blue agaves, orange-flowered Kaffir lilies, three jade trees, three ficus trees, and a 14-foot podocarpus, also known as a Buddhist Pine.

Along with the orchids I trained the passionflowers, which tended to grow to the ceiling of the greenhouse, wrapping around the fan blades, and root-pruned them when the roots crept through the bottom of the pot and wormed their way into the brick floor. Sometimes Jenna and I would prune back the podocarpus to keep it from slowly pressing against the ceiling and growing warped. We would lay it down across the greenhouse floor and warp it in a different way, lopping off apical buds so the growth pushed outward not upward. I fertilized the banana trees, urging them to flush out just one more glorious, person-sized leaf. Such was my routine, encouraging and taming, striking the balance between growth and nongrowth, and doing it in such a way that made it appear as though I'd never been there at all, as though this was some sort of spontaneous ecosystem that had sprung up through the bricks from the cold and damp New England soil.

2.

I had been working in the greenhouse for a few years before I really considered that to keep such a greenhouse collection was a centuries-old tradition. Who was responsible for giving rise to the Western world's obsession with "exotic" plants—plants, that is, from distant and unfamiliar climates and continents? Once I became aware of this question, I became curious about those who had the task of discovering them (for the Western world) in the first place—the explorers and naturalists who were sent on expeditions. The greenhouse gave me one story of the orchids, and narratives like Alexander von Humboldt's gave me another—a story set in a landscape where the flowers are wild and free. Of course, people in China and Japan had already been cultivating cymbidiums for centuries. In Bhutan, people eat cymbidium flowers in a curry. Those accounts fascinated me too. But I wanted to know the history responsible for the mass domestication of plants, where European wealth and obsession collided with still sparsely colonized land. Where occidental met oriental (*El Oriente* people in South America call the tropical rainforest of the Amazon basin). Where the Western mindset of conquest and ownership met with the wild, the unknown—what was then considered the allure of the exotic.

It was *Cymbidium violaceum* von Humboldt saw along the cataracts of the Atures River during his travels in South America. As I read through parts of his *Personal Narrative of Travels,* I kept looking for a detailed description of a single flower, particularly a cymbidium, looking for the one that perhaps he obsessed over. But he didn't obsess. Not over anything singular, anyway. Von Humboldt was one of the forerunners of the field of ecology, and he didn't look at a plant without looking at climate and altitude and the plants surrounding it or the people who interacted with it. He died just six months before Darwin published *On the Origin of Species,* and it's clear that Darwin likely would not have realized what he did if it weren't for the writings and previous observations of von Humboldt. Darwin carried *Personal Narrative* with him on the Beagle. "I formerly admired Humboldt, I now almost adore him," he wrote in a letter to a professor friend of his. And so I went to von Humboldt seeking orchids.

In *Personal Narrative*, von Humboldt writes: "I was passionately devoted to botany," but "the discovery of an unknown genus seemed to me far less interesting than an observation on the geographical relations of the vegetable world, or the migration of the social plants, and the limit of the height which their different tribes attain on the flanks of the Cordilleras."

In an article about von Humboldt, medical historian Malcolm Nicolson explains that around the turn of the nineteenth century, scientists' "legitimate objects of inquiry" generally tended toward "the aspects of nature that were clearly describable, in visual terms." The taxonomic system created by Carl Linnaeus some 50 years before had become the dominant method for scientific classification. Species were observed singularly and categorized by the makeup of their parts—how many petals, what kind of leaves—and given a series of names that could help the observer place the plant into its correct taxonomic position.

But von Humboldt and other natural historians like him were turning their attention to a more universal science, a *physique générale*. It was, according to Nicolson, "the universal science which would speak of the unity of nature and which was, to Humboldt, the chief end of all natural inquiry."

Von Humboldt's descriptions in his *Personal Narrative* are lively and observant, and he is just as interested in humans and culture as he is in the various species he's identifying. It doesn't feel like I'm reading science at all—it doesn't appear that he's traveling across the Western hemisphere to study and collect specimens but rather to explore and enjoy life. So whereas I came to *Personal Narrative* for the plants, I ended up staying for descriptions such as this, of humans interacting with the natural world:

> Despite the copious bleeding the little Indian girl swam ashore with her remaining arm. In those lonely places where man lives in constant struggle with nature he must resort to any means to fight off a jaguar, a boa . . . or a crocodile; everyone is prepared for some sort of danger. "I knew," said the young Indian girl coolly, "that the crocodile would let go when I stuck my fingers in its eyes."

Or his descriptions of the not-quite-humans in the natural world:

> It was at the cataracts that we first heard talk about the hairy man of the
> jungle, called *salvaje*, who rapes women, builds huts, and sometimes eats
> human flesh. Neither Indians nor missionaries doubt the existence of this
> man-shaped monkey, which terrifies them. Father Gili seriously related the
> story of a lady from San Carlos who praised the gentle character of the man
> of the jungle. She lived several years with him in great domestic harmony,
> and only asked hunters to bring her back home because she and her children
> (rather hairy also) "were tired of living far from a church."

I went seeking a flower and found an ecosystem within his narratives. If
I was looking for a description of orchids up close, I should have turned to the
Swedish botanist Olof Shwarz, or maybe Linnaeus, or even Darwin.

As it turns out, von Humboldt's *Cymbidium violaceum* was reclassified in
1889. Now it's part of the *Cattleya* genus—not a cymbidium at all. But by the
time I learned that, it almost didn't even matter anymore.

3.

I didn't want to be a gardener. It sort of happened by accident. In the summer
of 2005, I had finished an internship and I needed work. A friend had turned
down a job with Jenna and passed her name on to me. A few days later we met
up in an ice cream shop. She was a lean, wiry, and poised 27-year-old—only
two years older than me. She was a high school dropout, had been gardening
since she was a teenager, and had owned her own small business for a few
years already. She called it Viridissima—"greenest" in Latin—and her previous helper had moved away. Jenna took me on to help her finish up the
season—transplanting, digging up and storing tender perennials, cutting the
gardens back, and mulching for the winter. I still joke that the first things I
learned about gardening were "cut it all down and dig it all out."

It was supposed to be a temporary gig, a way for me to make some money
to get me back on my feet, to save up until I was ready to get on with what I
really wanted to do with my life. I had moved back to Massachusetts the
previous winter from Arizona, and it was somewhere in the back of my mind

to head west again. There was a plethora of ecological or biological research positions in the west that would require me to be where I wanted to be, out in the wilderness interacting with nature. I was searching for work that felt important. In Massachusetts, such jobs were hard to come by, and so I settled for gardening, which still allowed me to get dirty and sweaty and sunned.

Gardening didn't have the right sense of importance, though. The priorities were all wrong. As a gardener, I was only helping keep wealthy people's properties tidy and beautiful. I was doing the work because someone had enough money to pay me to do it—not because I believed it worthy or because of some greater ideological motive. As a naturalist or ecologist, I observed whole systems; each part responded to or was the result of interactions among other parts. Natural landscapes were intricate and symbiotic arrangements where flora and fauna had evolved of their own accord, free of humans. A garden was its own little system, but the relationship among the plants was a human construct, conformed to a theory of beauty, and that was inherently less interesting to me than what was wild.

The gardening, however, paid well. Much better than any environmental job, and Jenna was generous, raising my rate by a dollar an hour after my first month working for her, and then another dollar when I started up again the next spring. My rate increased steadily like this over the next few years, and I had a flexible schedule that didn't require any additional commitment—I only needed to show up. I've often tried to pinpoint the moment when I gave up—or gave in, I suppose—when I finally acknowledged that I had spent enough years longing to do something else and just accepted my vocation.

In summer at the mansion, while it was still unoccupied, we took the plants outside and arranged them by the pool. For six days a week, except for an occasional visit for watering, the plants kept each other company. The Kaffir lily bloomed in brilliant orange clusters just for the tadpoles and frogs that lived and died in the murk of the sagging pool cover. One spring a pair of mallards took up residence on the pool, taking advantage of its abandonment. Inside the pool house hung a No Trespassing sign. Beneath the line where the owner's name is meant to go, the previous owner had scrawled in black magic marker: "Trespassers will be shot!" The climbing hydrangea, seeking new light, crept down the lattice and across the stones of the patio, onto the screen of the pool house. Each year the pool furniture, also left by the previous owner, looked more like kindling, lichen growing in the gray and splintered grooves.

During certain years, I took better care of the plants than I did of myself, but such was my livelihood, like a horticultural nanny, attending to plants that fed on a seven-day regimen rich with nitrogen, potash, and potassium. Sometimes I took the cap off a tiny bottle of Superthrive and inhaled deeply, the salty richness like something I might sprinkle on brown rice or sip by the capful. Instead, I'd pour a dribble into a full watering can to give distressed plants an instant boost, like Gatorade after a soccer match. I'd eat my lunch alone in the courtyard garden, ripping up leaves of parsley or stalks of chive that nobody ever came to harvest and sprinkled them into my leftover pasta. I primped and pinched and turned and watered and fed, and the plants flowered gloriously for no one but me.

Every once in a while the owner, let's call him Jackson, did show up. He'd enter the greenhouse or the pool area, grin and look around. He seemed too young to be so wealthy—late 40s, maybe—and he had a warm, innocent face. He and his wife had two daughters; the wife had sea-green eyes, wild dark hair, and a kind of beauty that reminded me of Nick Carraway's description of a movie star at one of Gatsby's decadent parties: "a gorgeous, scarcely human orchid of a woman."

Jackson would say something like, "Look what you've done," or "I can't believe the way that passionflower is flowering!" He was utterly pleased with the property. One day he came in and said, "Look what I got for the crew," and held up a fleece vest with the name of the estate monogrammed below the left shoulder. The crew was Jenna and me, or whatever other workers she brought on each season, his landscaper, and sometimes the arborist who came to prune the arborvitae maze or cut down the occasional diseased tree. But we didn't really work together, each of us focusing on our respective spheres. We didn't feel like a "crew" to me.

Unlike other clients, Jackson remembered my name even though we'd met only a handful of times. The day he brought the vests, he sized me up and handed me a medium, and when I tried it on later I found it hung down nearly to my knees, the armholes showing half my ribcage. I kept it on a shelf for a week, then gave it to Jenna and told her to pass it on to another worker. I didn't doubt that Jackson might don his own fleece vest, blue right up to its collar, but when I put on mine, it felt like a badge denoting rank and class, putting me in my place.

Whereas Jackson was a cordial client who trusted me to do my work and even let me know that he appreciated my skills, there were clients we worked for who questioned my capabilities. With these clients, it was hard not to feel the class divide—I was the sweaty, tan, silent woman shoveling compost and transplanting azalea shrubs in their backyards; they talked on the phone, instructed their housekeepers, planned dinner parties, or ignored me altogether. Jenna, however, was always treated with utmost respect. She knew how to navigate their world even though she'd grown up poor. Whenever I asked her what a specific client did for a living, she'd shrug and say, "Manages his money?"

I watched several of her clients grow dependent on her, really come to need to have her around so that they could talk about all the changes they were going to make to their private landscapes. For some it had reached a level of desperation—they were going to get the *exact* shade of pink phlox to line their shrub border; they wanted to transplant their flowering lilies because they were too crowded, even though it was 90 degrees and precisely the wrong time to be transplanting; they wanted limbs pruned just so and privet sheared to a razor's edge; they just couldn't sit right unless the sedum showed a rosy blush instead of just being green. Jenna thrived on these little details because she could see what they saw, and she enjoyed finding plants that were unusual or interesting, that pleased the viewer in the right way. She was incredibly patient and very good at what she did. But there were those clients who just weren't happy no matter what, and they clung to Jenna's side, pointing and discussing all the things they would like to change, all the things that would finally make their property *perfect*. I came to believe that it wasn't the service we were giving them that made them satisfied, it was the process of eventually gaining complete control over their properties. It wasn't the way the landscape looked, but the way they envisioned it *eventually* looking, and there was always something next to conquer, which meant never being happy with the way things were.

Daphne was one of these clients. If I showed up at her house alone with a list of tasks, the first question was always, "When will Jenna be here?" Daphne followed me around, hovering over my shoulder. "Is that a weed that you're pulling?" "Are you sure that's a weed?" "Did Jenna tell you to do that?" "Did Jenna tell you that that's a weed?"

Even now when I meet Jenna for coffee, she likes to sneak up behind me as I get napkins or a stir stick: "Did Jenna tell you to take that napkin? Did Jenna tell you to sit down?" She says it faster and faster—"Did Jenna tell you? Did Jenna tell ya? Did genitalia?"—until we are cracking up and shaking our heads, "Oh, Daphne. It must be so hard."

Daphne's house and property were designed by Daniel Chester French, the artist who designed the Lincoln Memorial, and included a cement gazebo in the yard that Daphne called the summerhouse, where on one afternoon she invited the housekeeper and me to have a cold drink with her. We made small talk. "I can see exactly how Daniel Chester French positioned the summerhouse to catch the afternoon wind," she said. I was preparing a trip to Virginia the next day, and when I told Daphne she asked, "Oh, will you visit Monticello? I visit every time I'm that way. Jefferson kept the most beautiful gardens!" I told her no, I wouldn't have time, and what I really wanted to say was, of course he did—he kept just the right number of slaves to care for them all, too. But instead we sat in silence, watching the haziness of the afternoon settle over the canna lilies in her half-moon garden. A little while later she laughed and said, "Do you think Daniel Chester French would have ever imagined all us commoners sitting here like this?"

4.

What really bothered me about Jackson's fleece vest—an offering I honestly believe was made from his kindness and enthusiasm—was that it forced me to admit what I really was: a gardener. I became less a woman interested in plants, less a human curious about the natural world and all its rich complexities. I was just a gardener. The vest was a uniform, a garment that could allow anybody to size me up and categorize me and my place in this burgeoning re-creation of a mini-paradise. My biggest regret with being a gardener is perhaps the feeling, however real or however self-imposed, that had I lost control of my life, of who I believed myself to be.

When the explorers before von Humboldt started collecting plants and carrying them back to European kingdoms, everything was neatly categorized according to Linnaeus's taxonomic system. He did away with long, descriptive names of species, creating instead single-word classification systems. The system we use today to classify all biological life on earth has changed very little from Linnaeus's. All life is arranged into a taxonomic rank, given a name for each category, ranging from most general to most specific: kingdom, phylum, class, order, family, genus, species. Sometimes in considering a plant such as the greenhouse cymbidiums, I became the plant—uprooted from some sort of wild potential, no longer a woman setting forth to explore some untamed wilderness. Instead, like a potted cymbidium, I rested in my cordoned-off corner, my station determined by the namers, from the top down. Rather than tumbling endlessly over a rocky ledge out in the wild, year after year, I now had a name and position, one that kept me bound in place, just like a flower in one of the king's neatly categorized gardens.

Von Humboldt's expeditions were funded by King Charles IV of Spain, who gave him an open-ended passport for his journey to South America. The king's full name was Carlos Antonio Pascual Francisco Javier Juan Nepomuceno Jose Januario Serafin Diego, and perhaps with such grandiose traditions it's no wonder that his predecessor, King Charles III, who reigned during the Enlightenment period, became one of the biggest proponents of exploration and natural history collection. It was Charles III who started the Royal Academy of Fine Arts and the Royal Cabinet of Natural History. Over the entryway into the Royal Academy one can still read the Latin inscription: "King Charles III/united nature and art under one roof/for the public good/in the year 1774." Botanical expeditions had been happening long before the Enlightenment period—notably during the sixteenth and seventeenth centuries in the New World—but during this period right before the Napoleonic wars, Europe was sending naturalists across the world in the name of science. These expeditions had the appearance of being for the betterment of all people—enlightenment, I suppose—but Andrew Schulz, in *Spain in the Age of Exploration 1492–1819*, sees it differently: "After midcentury [1700s], much of the energy of Spanish science was directed toward fulfilling imperial ambition, as evidenced most overtly by scientific voyages to the New World often sponsored by the Royal Cabinet of Natural History. In the most general sense, such expeditions served the military mandate of knowing what one had and protecting it, and the economic one of figuring out how to best exploit it."

Throughout his life, Charles III held a certain passion for the natural world. He hunted. He kept a zoo and had a particular affinity for his elephants. In *Spain in the Age of Exploration*, I came across a painting of Charles as a child by Jean Ranc, done around 1725. The king-to-be wears red stockings, a royal blue dress embroidered lavishly with gold, lace peeking out from his cuffs. His hair tumbles down his back in fair curls, soft against his rosy-cheeked complexion. On the table before him is a vase full of morning glories, daffodils, roses, and tulips, and he holds a sprig of flowers in his right hand.

Later, as king, Charles III moved the original 2,000 specimens of the royal garden from the Orchard of Migas Calientes on the banks of the Manzanares River to where it still stands today at the Paseo del Prado—one of the main boulevards in Madrid. He augmented it with 10,000 more species collected by Italian explorer Alessandro Malaspina during his expedition around the world. He had the gardens formed into three-tiered terraces, and the plants arranged in squares according to Linnaeus's taxonomic system. "Thus, in addition to offering a pleasant, verdant oasis," Schulz continues, "the garden functioned as a representation of empire in miniature, gathering and organizing in the metropolis specimens found throughout the colonies and ordered according to the dictates of the latest European scientific methods of classification."

Von Humboldt's travels, and similar voyages that took place after his, were the natural results of Charles III's attempts to enlighten—from his desire to spread knowledge of the world, which is tied up with his obsession with wealth and ownership. When von Humboldt writes about the winged fruits of the *gyrocarpus* tree he found in Venezuela, and how he "sent some fruit to Europe, and they germinated in Berlin, Paris and Malmaison," I can't help but see kings' cravings for domination behind what otherwise appears to be a naturalist's passion for a specific tree. When I stood in the greenhouse and stared at the cymbidiums wondering, how did these plants end up *here*, I can, even if somewhat obliquely, trace their lineage back to Bourbon Spain and to the imperialistic urges burgeoning in young Charles's mind, deep beneath those golden locks.

Ranc's painting seems less about the king and more about an era. I know there must be some way to decode the placement of the objects, to read it as Man's dominion over nature. Perhaps it's the future king's feathered hat tossed carelessly behind him. Or perhaps it's the way a bird is perched in the shadows, compelling the viewer to lean in, or the confident expression on that young, cherubic face. He looks like Apollo, more god-like than human, the slight smile and the sprig of flowers ominous, as if he could ball up his fist and crush the delicate petals if he wished. But the cherub asks us to trust him, to believe he wouldn't ever do such a thing. Perhaps he's already dreaming of his empire in miniature. It's hard to know if, when the day comes, he will envision himself in it—in his many-tiered representation—or only above it, the classifier but never the classified.

5.

I recently rediscovered a photo of myself at 21. I'm crouched in the corner of the picture, looking over my shoulder at the camera. I have a bandana on my head, and it's only after I've examined the photo closely that I remember my hair was short. I'd shaved my head the previous year, my first stab at trying to identify as someone other than who I'd always been. That summer I was trying to grow it out but was facing the humiliation a curly-haired person faces when the hair reaches the clown-wig phase. Before me spreads a field of cotton grass, thousands of white tufts, and beyond that is the Slims River, and beyond that a vast and bulking mountain range, jagged and snow capped. Only once I flip it over do I remember that the photo was taken in Kluane National Park in Canada's Yukon Territory. I was taking a summer field course (most of it in Alaska), and on the back of the photo, which must have been destined for my parents, I wrote that the cotton grass is really a sedge. I remember learning how to feel the stem for squareness—sedge is square, rush is round. I end the note by writing, "This is me being a Naturalist, keying the plant out," as though even eleven years ago I had the sense that I played many roles in life, trying on various titles like hats, and I was playing naturalist, but I wasn't *a Naturalist* yet.

I spent that summer in places like Kluane and in the Brooks Range of Alaska. I kayaked in Prince William Sound and took a canoe trip up the

Tanana River, gray and murky from glacial silt. I remember identifying alpine plants, learning how over a certain latitude plants tend to have red foliage because of the angle of the sun, and thus the amount of sunlight they absorb over an Arctic summer. I remember crouching and looking at various species of gentian and arnica and finding them so stunning, something so small and perfect in a territory that still felt raw and recent as the last of the Ice Age melted away, and I was at a point in my life where I had as much potential as the changing landscape; surely, I thought, I was on the verge of something great and wonderful. Perhaps I didn't feel so different from von Humboldt on the eve of his journey to South America in 1799: "What attracted me about the torrid zone was no longer the promise of a wandering life full of adventures, but a desire to see with my own eyes a grand, wild nature rich in every conceivable natural product, and the prospect of collecting facts that might contribute to the progress of science."

Years later, planting a different species of gentian at Daphne's, I remember having that momentary start looking at the plant, captivated by the indigo of its petals. But the wonder was short-lived as I planted it near a patch of pachysandra, beneath a dwarf weeping cherry tree, interspersed with unusual colors of Echinacea flowers, and underplanted with a chartreuse groundcover called *Lysimachia nummularia* "Aurea," also known as Creeping Jenny, one of Jenna's favorites, which created a web of solid color and texture beneath the other plants. There was certainly satisfaction in looking at the arrangement—the colors and shapes, the way they filled that particular niche of land (a slope of a hillside with a few embedded boulders). Jenna had a way of constructing microcosms that felt simultaneously natural yet dissonant. I also remember a tinge of sadness because the gentian brought me back to Alaska and to a time in my life where I was certain that my future included exploration.

Plants are often a reminder of the various places I have been or could have been (*Begonia boliviensis* that I could have seen on mountainsides of Bolivia, the Angel Trumpet trees that I did see growing along rivers in Ecuador), and with them came the slight feeling of failure, that instead of being in these various places I was here, rearranging the natural world in a way that Daphne desired. To see all these plants from various places assembled together in Daphne's yard was like dismembering one of von Humboldt's physical "regions."

It's possible I was overly dramatic about it.

Nonetheless, these sorts of realizations are what kept me trying to get away from gardening year after year, kept me reminding myself that I wanted something more or nobler (Explorer! Writer!)—the sort of position in life that would keep me poor, and therefore kept me returning to gardening. I think maybe the question I really wanted to ask as I gazed on the cymbidiums was how did *I* end up here?

There's something to be said about the fact that people like Daphne will never be content with the pink of their pansies, and that despite all my cold feet about being a gardener, Jenna found me reliable enough that every February she'd send me an e-mail asking, "So, what are your plans for the summer?" If anything, they kept me busy. That's for sure.

"You're good at this, you know," Jenna said to me. "Why don't you just be a gardener?"

Some time after I repotted the cymbidiums, Jackson and his family slowly began to move to the mansion property. They moved into the caretaker's cottage, using the room above the greenhouse as a storage space and office. No pet elephants, like Charles III had on his premises, but they kept guinea pigs in the bathroom, a turtle in the office. Down in the barns were bunnies and cats and a pen filled with guinea hens and peacocks—both white and green—whose whooping, humanish cries lifted up across the manicured lawn, over the arborvitae maze into the open door of the greenhouse.

Recently, I happened upon a field of flowers in the wild. It was the morning of a good friend's wedding, and she wanted to pick the lupines for center arrangements. It was cold and misty, and the flowers grew wild by the hundreds of thousands in an open field at the base of Blue Hill Mountain in Maine. Through the coastal fog, we waded in knee-high wet grass, and when we came upon the lupines, fields and fields of them, my heart leapt—so strange, so beautiful, as exotic as rare orchids. They were up to my waist, and each flower stalk was loaded with hundreds of small asymmetrical flowers, each like a tiny pouch, like a miniature snapdragon. The flower stalks came to a conical point, and at the top, the flower buds were still closed tight, the flowers blooming from the bottom up. We were supposed to pick only enough—but I became greedy. I *needed* at least one that was a deep violet, one that was blue and white, one that was just white, one that was pink at the top fading to purple. I picked too many. We laid them in the trunks of our cars and brought them back; we arranged them in pottery vases that my friend had made, some bouquets so tall and resplendent that people took them off the tables during dinner in order to look across at people they hadn't seen in years. At dinner I sat next to an old college friend, eight months pregnant, who had once worked as a landscape gardener but now ran a restaurant. "I loved the plants, but I hated working for the rich people," she said as she picked at her dinner and rubbed her belly.

The next morning the lupines drooped listlessly, their peppery fragrance like a fog in the room, one last desperate attempt to communicate with the outside world. The smell unfurling from its nestled position within the flowers, like a call out to all the pollinators. As we folded tables and collected champagne bottles and nursed our burgeoning hangovers, I felt mild regret at my own greediness, at our mistake of having too many lupines. I also knew our bouquets hadn't made even a dent in the field of wild flowers. And whereas I can never recreate that initial moment of seeing them for the first time, of watching their form slowly take shape through the fog, of startling at the realization of just how many there were, that's the memory that sticks with me the most: the field of lupines. And I'll always prefer them like that, in the ripe moment before I even realized my urge to pick them, before my hand had touched them, and the rain droplets still rested like a mosaic of perfect beads upon the leaves.

Crush

MICHELLE PILAR HAMILL

A sketch of a wanted man hung on a corkboard at the corner of 96th and Amsterdam, in the Grand Union grocery store where my mother shopped. He looked like Alfred E. Neuman on the cover of my cousin's *MAD* magazines, but this man sodomized children. Soon most of the stores in the neighborhood had tacked up his likeness, until I couldn't keep track of all the places he was. I saw him near the registers at the Woolworth's, his picture splashed with purple grape juice. He was taped to the door at the Dairy Queen, home of my favorite cherry-dipped soft-serve. The dry cleaner framed his face beside headshots of his actor customers, but his was the only one that wasn't smiling.

At this dry cleaners, I learned what sodomy was. A woman, first in line, clutched a wedding dress trimmed with lace and tiny seed pearls. She was correcting the Korean storeowner who, knowing little English, thought sodomy meant the wanted man was cutting up children.

"That's *sawing*. Not sodomy," said the woman, shifting the weight of her white dress.

The dry cleaner scrunched his brow. "*What*?" he asked.

"This man is wanted for snatching up little kids and doing them up the butt without their say-so," she said, deliberately, as if teaching a preschool class.

A seamstress, tucked in a space behind the washing machines, stopped mid-stitch. All you could hear were shirts being pressed in the background. The dry cleaner clapped his hands above his head and the ironing came to a standstill, the last puffs of steam rising to the ceiling. He shook a metal hanger at the woman. "You are *crazy*," he said.

"No, I'm right." And with that, she dropped her wedding dress on his counter. "I can't look at this thing hanging in my closet another second. Store it. Charge me. I'll be back for it *never*."

The dry cleaner stared back at her. Remembering what he was there for, he took a pen from his shirt pocket and wrote her a receipt. When the lady turned to leave she found me standing a foot and a half below her with an armful of dirty clothes almost as big as I was.

"Oh. Hello," she said, somewhat rattled. "All of those yours?"

"They're my mother's," I told her. "She's an actress."

"I see," she said, staring at the lump of laundry I was struggling to hold. "And where is she now?"

"At the drugstore buying Pssst."

"What in the world?"

"It's dry shampoo for last-minute auditions."

"You don't say?" She pulled on the belt of her navy jacket. Her eyes were mostly white and unblinking, round and smudged with black eyeliner. "Maybe I'll just wait for her. There *is* a crazy man on the loose." She stuck her hands deep into her pockets and headed for a rack of New York City souvenir postcards that the dry cleaner sold on the side. "I'm right over here until she turns up," she said.

I was always waiting for my mother, but it was strange to have someone else waiting with me.

A carousel of clean clothes in clear plastic started turning. I watched a kelly green coat with large gold buttons going round and round. Across the room, the woman who knew about sodomy collected postcards of the Empire State Building, Rockefeller Center, and Times Square. When she picked a card she liked, she called out "Little girl!" and held it up to show it to me.

The kelly green coat was on its eighth lap when my mother hurried in. The bell on the door jingled, as if to accompany my happiness upon seeing her. She'd been gone less than 15 minutes but it was rare to have her return so soon. The dry cleaner smiled and waved, excited as I was to see her. Last time we were in, he'd told her she was as pretty as the girls on *The Dating Game* and that she should give them a call and get on the show.

"Hi, sweetie, let me take those," my mother said, scooping her clothes from my arms and handing me a packet of cherry-flavored Chiclets.

"Mamma's little helper," beamed the dry cleaner, more at my mother than at me.

"Yes, she is," said my mother, unwrapping the butterscotch she took from a cut-glass bowl on the counter. The dry cleaner watched as she placed the candy into her mouth. She showed him a stain on one of her silk blouses.

"No problem. I have that out in a super flash," he said, sliding her dirty clothes out of her arms. "You have *beautiful* things. *Very* good taste. *This* I can tell."

I had lost track of the woman watching over me by the postcards when suddenly she appeared. Mesmerized by my mother and the smitten dry cleaner, she chewed on her bottom lip, as if whatever they were doing made her terribly sad. I wondered if it had something to do with her wedding dress and how she didn't want it anymore.

She turned and was once again startled upon seeing me. Squinting in my direction, it was as if she'd already forgotten who I was. She put on a pair of giant black sunglasses and leaned down to me. "Don't you worry about that bad man," she whispered. "He's only after little boys."

As she left, the door jingled again, this time sounding like the ushering in of something terrifying, something I thought I couldn't keep away.

After the dry cleaner finished sorting through my mother's garments, we headed off to buy groceries at the Grand Union. I liked going shopping with my mother. It meant an evening of her undivided attention, where she taught me things like which detergent worked best and to buy only orange juice from Florida.

But before we had a chance to get there she was looking at her watch. I knew what was coming.

"Oh shoot, I really have to get to the theater," she said. "Could you go to the store without me, honey? We only need a couple of things." She was already in her purse, searching for her wallet. "You know, when I was ten, I *loved* going to the store by myself."

"I'm eight," I said.

"But you'll be nine in three months. It's just around the corner."

A man across the street was walking toward us. He smiled at my mother and moved on. I wanted to ask her about the wanted man, like if they had caught him, but didn't want to keep her from where she had to go.

"Or we could just wait until later in the week," she said, "but then you'll be out of strawberry Pop-Tarts."

I loved strawberry Pop-Tarts, but now I was thinking about the wanted man's poster tacked up on the "community board" just beyond the first entrance of the grocery store. I had been able to avoid the sketch of his face at the dry cleaners because he and the actors' headshots were hung high on a wall above the cash register. The wanted poster at the grocery store was hard to miss. If my mother came with me I could take her hand and close my eyes until we were safely inside the market.

Instead I took her grocery list and money and watched her head off down the street without me. I looked up at the sun and wondered how long it would stay there, hoping it wouldn't get dark anytime soon.

Entering the grocery store, I did what I could to avoid the sketch of the wanted man: the gap in his front teeth, his pug nose, and his small eyes looking back at me.

The corkboard with his picture was cemented to the wall between the supermarket's two electric doors, a kind of way station where they stored the shopping carts. I was only getting a few things, was too small to push one anyway, so I hurried through the first electric door, aiming for the second. I was pretty sure I could hear the wanted man breathing, that at any moment he would spring to life. I stared straight ahead, into the supermarket, keeping my eyes on the pyramid displays of creamed corn, dish soap, and dog biscuits.

That's when I realized the second electric door wasn't opening. I stepped a little harder on the black mat, right in the place that read *Step Here*. Still the door wouldn't budge. I wondered if I was too light, or worse, no longer present. Untethered to the earth, I'd floated away, and that's why the door hadn't noticed me.

I walked right up to the door. Since I wasn't there I could pry it open and remain unharmed. It opened just a little, enough for me to slide my hand in. I was gone. I was a ghost. I could do that. But then the door closed. I pulled my hand back, but it managed to catch my thumb and slowly crush it. I felt it take hold, tighten, then move beyond that, inflicting a pain I'd yet to conceive of. I screamed. The door opened again. I kept screaming thinking the door could hear me, that this was the reason it had opened. Then I turned and found an old man standing on *Step Here*. I saw his two-wheeled grocery cart. How he leaned into it, as if without it he would fall. I noticed his milky gray eyes, the hand that was reaching for me, his pajama top with cowboys and horses peeking out from the bottom of his tweed jacket. Then the things I saw began to spin out from under me, my mother's grocery list spiraling in the air above, as I dropped in a clump to the floor.

Somewhere inside the whirl I thought about the old man, wondering if he had any grandchildren. I saw the face of my grandfather, a Whitman's Sampler box perched on his lap, watching *The Waltons* on TV, his mono-grammed golf clubs propped against his plaid recliner. Silent, as always. Like the portrait of my grandmother's father that hung over their fireplace, painted in coattails, holding a glass of champagne, a gold pocket watch dangling from his shirt front. My mother said he'd fallen in love with a much younger woman, which saddened my great-grandmother so much she died from a broken heart. Maybe that's why my mother was quick to leave the men she married.

When I fell to the floor I traveled into a darkness that poured me into a silver fish-bowl, before breaking like an egg into bright white. I came to looking up at the fluorescent globe-like fixtures that hung from the ceiling of the supermarket. Music flowed from the loudspeaker, something about hav-ing someone's baby and what a wonderful way it was of saying how much she loved him.

Drifting back into my body, I found myself curled inside a red leather chair big enough to hold most of me. It was worn, split in several places, with foam clouds spilling out from every wound. I had never seen this chair before. You had to be stationed behind the butcher's glass display case—as I was—to know it existed. My thumb was wrapped in gauze but still bled through. I was woozy. My head throbbed, light, dark, light, dark, as I slipped in and out of consciousness.

I hadn't yet noticed the three butchers that worked in the meat depart-ment, or that the youngest one held up my injured hand. Then I saw his chewed-down fingernails and the tattooed snake in emerald green climbing up his ring finger.

His face was turned away from mine, focused on the other two butchers who were too hazy for me to see. He said, "The only fix for this shit is a motherfucking butterfly stitch. Anything else is just pussy."

"Yo. Whoa. *Language*," said the older butcher stepping in closer to me. Husky and weathered, he spoke and the other butchers paid attention.

"Sorry, boss. I've just been cut up more times than I'd like to tell you. See this?" He let go of my hand to pull up his shirtsleeve. My hand hit the armrest and I let out a scream.

"Oh shit, she's awake!" said the youngest butcher as the other two rushed in.

There was no way I could greet them; I was rising up like a balloon toward the beige, stuccoed ceiling. I saw the electric door and the picture of the wanted man leaning out from his flyer, turning his eyes on me.

I woke again to another voice saying, "Don't you worry, sweetheart, the ambulance will be here any minute." Kneeling before me was the third butcher. He was beautiful, like a Latino David Cassidy. I had been a card-carrying member of *The Partridge Family* Fan Club since first grade. Forget the head injury and bleeding finger, his beautiful face was the factor that almost did me in.

"My cousin Ricky got shot last week, took 'em half an hour to arrive," said the youngest butcher.

"Will you shut the fuck up, Patrick?" said the handsome one, adding, "*Please*," as if to make up for his cursing.

The older butcher came into focus, "How you doing, honey?"

"Screw the ambulance," said the youngest butcher, back on his soapbox. "We could do a monumentally better job right here. They got small needles in housewares."

"Hey. Whoa. Silence," said the older butcher.

"Right. Sorry, little girl." He stopped for a moment, but then couldn't help himself. "I'm just saying, they don't know jack shit. This here is the real deal." He grabbed a headless chicken for emphasis. "We got our hands in blood and guts every day. I could sew the head back on this poor bastard, have him walking in no time."

The three butchers erupted in laughter, fake-punched the youngest one still holding the headless bird.

"Yeah, right. You certainly missed your calling," said the handsome one.

"E-*nough*," said the older butcher, before turning his attention to me. "Don't listen to those knuckleheads. They've got screws loose." But he said it in a way that showed how he really liked them. He put his rough hand on my arm. It was cold and flecked with cow's blood, but I didn't mind.

In the distance I heard a siren. I didn't want it to get any closer. I wanted to stay in the red chair, with the butchers. The light in the room was warm on my face. The music from the loudspeaker almost drowned out the siren. *Having my baby, what a wonderful way of saying how much you love me.* It was the same song I'd heard when I woke the first time, but it didn't seem to be ending. *Didn't have to keep it, wouldn't put you through it. You could have swept it from your life, but you wouldn't do it.* My head dipped down and I righted it.

More distant than the siren was the voice of the handsome butcher. "Hey, sweetheart," he asked, "where's your mom and dad?"

I wanted to tell him about my mother's pale hands. How she was always the love interest in every play she acted in, the type of woman that men wanted to sing "*having my baby*" to. She was a trail of curlers dropped throughout the house, getting ready for an audition, attached to nothing but the straw in her Carnation Instant Breakfast. At home or at work she was always so far away. Too far for me to tell her about the wanted man who appeared up and down the block where we lived, climbing to my window, hiding behind trees and breaking off their blossoms, turning the knob on our front door, making his way inside.

The music drifted back in. Elton John was now singing over the loudspeaker, wondering when we were going to come down, when were we going to land? The shoppers rolled their carts a little slower, as if they were thinking about this very question.

The handsome butcher was still with me. "Keep your hand up, sweetheart. It'll stop the bleeding."

"My mother's in a play at The Public Theater."

"Oh, *yeah*? Fancy."

"What's The Public Theater?" asked the youngest butcher.

"A very *prestigious* organization," I said, just as I'd heard my mother call it.

"Exactly. Get some culture, why don't you?" said the handsome one.

"The play's called *Siamese Connections*," I said. The shoppers started to pick up speed; I felt dizzy and looked away, straight into the handsome butcher's eyes.

"Like the double pipes or the people?" he asked.

"I don't know," I said, sorry not to have an answer for him. He seemed drawn to my story, which both thrilled and unnerved me. "There's a pig that gets killed in it." This I hoped would keep his interest.

"No kidding?"

"Well, not really. My mother's understudy does the squealing from off-stage."

"Yeah, well around here we've got the real deal," said the youngest butcher. He pointed to their display case of meat, to the dozen or so pigs' feet placed in a perfect row, framed in a parsley garnish.

"Poor pigs," I said, softly, as if they could hear me.

"Which one?"

"All of them," I said, looking through the display case, wondering where their heads went.

"They don't feel a thing, honey," said the handsome one.

A twinge rippled through my hand. Then my head.

"Yeah, once you take their feet, they're pretty much dead," said the youngest, running his finger across his neck. Someone grabbed him by the shoulders and shoved him aside. My thumb ached. The pain that had been missing snapped into focus. I tried not to cry but my sight blurred over in warm tears.

The older butcher returned. "Get her a Kleenex, you imbecile. And no more pig talk!"

"I was just trying to distract her," said the youngest one, handing me a tissue, his eyebrows raised like a scolded puppy.

"What else happens in this play?" asked the handsome butcher with the small scar that cut like a tiny lightning bolt across his eyebrow.

Before I could answer, an announcement broke over the store's loud speaker: corn on the cob, half price.

"Oh yeah?" said the youngest butcher, about to shed his white apron and run for the sale.

"Stay there," ordered the older butcher. The youngest butcher slumped down onto a wood stool, crossed his arms, and made a sad face.

I thought I flew above the store. From there I could see Grand Union's customers running for the vegetable aisle, filling up their carts with cheap corn. I followed them home where they shucked the green husks and found the yellow kernels, throwing them into pots to boil.

Then I returned to the red chair to tell the butchers another thing I remembered about my mother's play: how the family in it celebrates a son's birthday with candles and a cake while on the other side of the stage he is away at war, being shot up by the enemy. The family blows out his candles and cheers, unaware that at that very same moment he is dying.

The butchers were quiet.

Until the youngest one broke the silence. "That's fucked up," he said.

In the distance I heard another siren.

"Bet that's for you," said the handsome one, as if it were a good thing. I didn't want it to be for me. The butchers circled around the red chair; I wanted to stay here forever.

"My mother plays the fiancé of the man who dies."

"The love interest?"

"Uh huh," I said, embarrassed by the thought of it. "But after he dies she falls in love with his brother."

My head crisscrossed with thoughts about other men: My father who came over from Cuba when he was a little boy. And my Israeli ex-stepfather who'd moved here as a young man. Where were they now? Had they returned to the places they once had lived?

The youngest butcher moved into my sightline. "Wait. You mean she got with the brother, with her husband just shot dead and all?"

The siren drew closer, louder than any other sound in the market. Then it stopped. The store stood still in a temporary hush. And the music swept in again.

"They're coming for you, little girl," said the handsome butcher.

"Will there be firemen?" I asked.

"Why, you on fire?" he asked, smiling. "I don't think so."

My mother's last boyfriend was a fireman. I knew this because of the shiny gold badge he pinned to the pocket of his stiff white shirt. He told me a story about a man who'd been thrown from a motorcycle, whose face collapsed like a pancake when he went to administer mouth-to-mouth, because every bone had broken. I wanted to ask him if they were able to put the man back together, or if not, how he lived with a broken face. But the fireman had left after his story, and I had not seen him since.

Up the center aisle of the grocery store ran two men in dark blue jump suits. One of them carried a large white case. Neither was the fireman I once knew. When they reached the meat section the butchers formed a barricade in front of me to block them. Only after checking their badges did the butchers step aside.

I fell into the chair, below the red leather, deep inside the foam clouds and stayed there while the paramedics stuck me with a needle, removed the butcher's bandages, and dressed my injuries once again. They took my pulse and temperature, lifted me out of the chair, and placed me onto the gurney. My thumb became the center of everything, pounded as if it were still caught in the electric door.

"The pain should ease up any second now," said the paramedic, strapping me onto the gurney.

"Do you know where my mom is?" I asked, but he was busy packing up his white case, writing things down on his clipboard.

The butchers gathered around to say their goodbyes.

"Hang in there, sweetheart, you hear?" said the older butcher.

"Looks like you'll live, kid," said the youngest one with a shy smile.

The handsome butcher came into view. A gold chain had slid from the top of his white apron, so the cross swung back and forth over my body. "Don't worry about a thing. And you be sure and come round, show us your stitches. Got to make sure they did a good job." He rubbed the top of my head and tapped a gentle punch against my cheek.

The paramedics wheeled me away. I watched as the butchers returned to work, showing steaks to their customers, wrapping them in white paper, pulling a black crayon from behind one ear and jotting down a price. The last thing I saw was the older butcher reaching across the silver counter of their shining display case, handing over a package of meat to a lady with a baby carriage. He looked up and caught my gaze just as I turned the corner.

I tried to remember my father, but I couldn't recall his face. Just the building we had lived in on Riverside Drive when he and my mother were still married. I remembered the wind that would sweep up the street, almost lifting me. And the super who doubled as the elevator man, riding me down to the basement, and telling me a monster lived behind the water heater. He said the roar and heat of the furnace was really just the monster, and since he had keys to all the apartments nothing could stop him from coming in. Then he took me back upstairs, opened the elevator door, and dropped me off. I didn't tell my mother. He said if I did, the monster would know. Or maybe he didn't say that, maybe I thought to tell her would only make her as scared as I was.

The paramedics rolled me around another corner, down the condiment aisle. I saw the ketchups, mustards, and relishes rising off the shelves and coming for me, while the pickles swam in jars of vinegar, wanting to escape. I thought of the tiny stillborn creatures my science teacher kept in jelly jars, floating in clear fluid stored on a high ledge in our classroom. I didn't understand what had happened to them, or how they ended up at our school. I stared at them for too long, until the class had moved on without me, their beakers bubbling, breaking out in billows of blue smoke, and I didn't know how I would ever catch up.

The last thing I saw as the paramedics wheeled me out of the grocery store was the sketch of the wanted man stepping right out of his flyer. The butchers were all over him. Took him by the collar and dragged him away.

After the ambulance left me at the hospital and the nurses had checked me in, my mother showed up. She ran in, looking like a lost child. She found me in the emergency room behind a curtain, lying on a bed, in a mint green robe much too big for me. The doctor came by and told her what had happened, how I'd crushed my thumb at the Grand Union and it was a miracle the bone in the finger was still intact, that I had fallen to the floor and hit my head, had been in and out of consciousness, which served to lessen most of the pain.

When the doctor went deeper into detail, about the cut, the blood, the cauterizing, my mother began to wince, telling him she didn't want to hear any more.

"I'm sorry. I just hate *hospitals* . . . There's so much sadness here." She waved her hand in front of her mouth, the same way she did in the play she was acting in each night after finding out her husband had died.

On the way home she bought me some peppermint Chiclets and a $100,000 Bar. She said I could stay home from school the rest of the week if I wanted.

The next day I used my good hand to transfer my blankets and pillow to the comfiest chair in the living room, reclining it to its most horizontal position. I searched through the *TV Guide*, planning my television strategy for the day of long ago reruns: *I Love Lucy. Gomer Pyle. The Brady Bunch.* I noted the bad shows I would have to suffer through (*F Troop, Hogan's Heroes*) to get to the good stuff: *The Partridge Family* (which I would never again see in the same way) and *I Love Lucy* again.

I heard my mother milling around, and just for a moment, I wondered if she had gotten up early just for me. When she appeared in the hallway of the living room, I saw her hair was already curled. She wore a white linen dress with a pale blue flower stitched above her heart. A warmth pushed at the surface of my chest and moved to my arms that wanted to reach for her. I stuck my uninjured thumb into my rib cage, just below my heart, then into my mouth, and reached instead for my blanket, thankful that the door had only crushed my non-sucking thumb.

"How are you feeling, honey?" my mother asked, coming over to place her cool hand onto my forehead. "No fever. You'll be fine," she said before I could answer.

She had her little blue book called "Heal Your Body" written by a Church of Religious Science disciple, the practice my mother was currently following. The book listed ailments, their deeper causes, and the metaphysical affirmations that would heal them.

"Let's see. Thumb. Thumb. Thumb," she repeated, looking for the psychological reason behind my crushed finger. "Here it is, 'represents intellect and worry.' Huh. Have you been thinking too much?" she asked me. I didn't know how to answer, shrugged my shoulders. "Sounds like you have been. So here's your affirmation: 'My mind is at peace.' Okay? Say it several times throughout the day: 'My mind is at peace.' Do that, and you'll be better in no time."

She told me there was orange juice, and I should drink a lot of it. Said to call her answering service if I needed her but she would try to check in between her back-to-back auditions. She said all this while being drawn to the TV, to Lucy getting into trouble with Desi.

"God. She was absolutely brilliant. Desi paled in comparison."

"This is a funny one," I said, wanting my mother to stay a little longer.

She sat on the edge of the couch near me.

"You know, Lucy took her props very seriously? She'd work with them for hours, *days*, until they felt just right."

For a couple more minutes I shared my mother with Lucy's brilliance. Her hand rested on my knee, but it was Lucy keeping her in the room.

At the first commercial, she got up to leave. Leaning down she kissed me on the cheek, her shiny hair resting on my face, and then lifting away.

"I've been thinking," she said, taking her headshot portfolio off the dining room table. "We should really start celebrating Father's Day. After all, I'm not only your mother now, I'm your father too."

The first time I returned to the Grand Union, the butchers threw their hands up and hollered things like, "Hey, little girl, how's it hanging? Your finger that is!" Then they laughed and called me over to inspect my bandages. They told me they would teach me their secret handshake once the stitches came out, and my thumb had healed to their liking. They said it was a handshake that only the meat section knew. Like if I tried it with the fruit guy he'd just crinkle up his nose and go back to stacking apples. They didn't know me in produce the way the butchers did. I belonged beneath the sign that read *Boneless cut, Shank cut, Porter cut, Prime.*

If I dreamed about the wanted man climbing up to my window, on waking, I'd picture the red leather chair, the butchers standing around it like soldiers at the gate. For a while I had something to soothe me, to put me back to sleep.

When the bandages were removed, the next day I ran from the bus to the Grand Union. The butchers inspected my stitches, admitting the doctor had done an okay job. The older butcher said they better have or they would have given him a what for. Then they pretended to be punching out the doctor, as if I was someone they wanted to protect.

When the doctor said my hand was good enough to use I went back to the Grand Union eager to learn my new handshake. But I learned that day that the youngest butcher got fired. And one week later the handsome one quit. The supermarket soon hired two new butchers and the older butcher was busy training them. He looked sad, as if he was missing something he couldn't get back. He never taught me the handshake, and after a while he stopped waving.

I still went to the store with my mother. And sometimes I went alone. But I stayed away from the meat department. It was just another thing that no longer belonged to me.

Commentary on "Crush":

IN SEARCH OF A SEAMLESS REFLECTION

MICHELLE PILAR HAMILL

I read *Crime and Punishment* fresh out of high school. Two-thirds through came a scene about a gang of heartless town folk who amused themselves by piling onto a horse-drawn cart while the driver whipped the horse to go. The load was too large, the horse too frail, the people howling with laughter as the horse struggled to obey. So pained was I by Dostoyevsky's brutal imaginings, I threw the book across the room and never opened it again. Even now the mere memory of this passage makes my lungs ache in a way I can only compare to grief. What disturbs me is that the horse can't understand what is happening, is being harmed by an oblivious force, and is facing the dark alone.

Just last week I tried to explain to my sister why I would not be making the six-hour drive with my husband and ten-month-old baby girl to Vermont for Thanksgiving. I said next year we'll go when she is cognizant of the journey. No, it probably won't make her time strapped to a car seat any easier, but at least she will have a greater awareness of why she is being subjected to such a trek.

There's a pattern here.

I project into the minds of animals and the very young. The reason is easy to find. Any first-year therapist could connect the dots at session one: I was born into a legacy of loneliness, raised with loss and upheaval, and left to my own devices to figure things out.

Now I've gone and told you something.

But in writing "Crush," I set out to keep my analysis under wraps.

That meant leaning toward a seamless reflection, which fused with the action, so unobtrusive it would live inside the story like a wraith. Hindsight was omnipresent but discreet, a shrewd whisperer in the reader's ear. There would be no "Looking back now," or "I eventually came to realize," phrases that could pull readers out of a world I wish for them to enter. I aimed to write from a place before understanding, to inhabit the child's confusion, and to speak from there.

In practice the girl's perception becomes center stage, seeing in a pointed way my orchestration. Once told, there should be symbolism in the furniture, emotion in the drapes. Everything has meaning. Pig's feet. Tiny stillborn creatures floating in jelly jars. Nothing is random. The girl will tell you what you need to know.

I write: "I wondered if I was too light, or worse, no longer present. Untethered to the earth, I'd floated away, and that's why the door hadn't noticed me." According to pediatrician and psychoanalyst Donald Winnicott, there's a reason the girl felt this way. He writes about the "holding environment": how the mother's embrace tells the baby that she is real, that she exists, and that her feelings and actions have meaning. Without this "gathering together," the child feels as if she is literally flying apart.

This is a sensation familiar to me.

Still, Winnicott won't make a cameo appearance in "Crush." He won't step out from the margins and explain the little girl's mindset. Instead, there's the thumb she sucks past an acceptable age or pushes into her rib cage to tell her she's there, the red chair she finds comfort in that's big enough to hold almost all of her, or the butchers who gather round and attend to her that I will enlist to evoke the unheld child.

In lieu of summary, let me drop down into long-ago places, look about, and gather the clues that bring forth a sense of isolation.

I write: "I heard my mother milling around, and just for a moment, I wondered if she had gotten up early just for me. When she appeared in the hallway of the living room, I saw her hair was already curled. She wore a white linen dress with a pale blue flower stitched above her heart. A warmth pushed at the surface of my chest and moved to my arms that wanted to reach for her. I stuck my uninjured thumb into my rib cage, just below my own heart, then into my mouth, and reached instead for my blanket, thankful that the door had only crushed my non-sucking thumb."

I am drawn to recreate a palpable loneliness, to show how I longed for an absent mother, "her shiny hair resting on my face, and then lifting away."

And what of the butchers and their paternal pull? Why did sitting behind their gleaming display case feel to the girl like protective armor? Today I can tell you: My father had all but faded from memory, a stepfather I'd come to call Daddy was MIA, and a parade of my mother's boyfriends was marching in and out of her, and consequently my, ever-changing life. Men were a mystery, a series of ghosts.

Therein lies the challenge of a seamless reflection in prose. How can I convey these layers of backstory without the girl or her grown-up counterpart spelling it all out whole hog?

Enter the rambling thoughts of a baffled eight-year-old with no frame of reference by which to fully comprehend. Then, inside the things she says or thinks about I'll punch the imprint of a lost girl.

For example, I set out to convey the girl's desire to communicate her mounting fears to the butchers. Sorting through my index cards of happenings around this same time, I remembered a play in which my mother was performing where a soldier gets killed onstage while his unknowing family sings *Happy Birthday* to him from thousands of miles away. The play—along with so many other plays my mother acted in—was fraught with inescapable emotion and complex portrayals of adult relationships that shot right over my third-grader head. It struck me that the disembodied and overwhelming feelings I sometimes had, alone in the darkness watching my mother act, mirrored my state outside the theater. It seemed then that the motivation for telling the butchers about this strange play was to somehow get at the larger question, *What the heck is going on?* Including this moment was one way I used to illuminate the girl's unrest.

Draft after draft, I struggled with telling too little or too much. I certainly didn't want to be cryptic, only that the reader might be the one to intuit what the girl could not articulate.

In time, a child can develop an analytical mind and give meaning to her experiences. Right or wrong, it will be the prism she will see through for decades to come, cast into broken horses and her own baby girl. Until then, she will gather the whirl of information, seek to bring it close and hold it, shape it within her small hands. Enter here.

Locate Mercy

LEONORA SMITH

You cannot separate passion from pathology.

No matter how many books you love, only one or two will love you back. To reread Richard Selzer's *Letters to a Young Surgeon* is to remind myself that I believe in synchronicity, and that when you are *in extremis,* when you have exhausted every resource, there is a book somewhere that will reteach you what you already know: that you can reverse the breaking and begin to knit your sundered parts. And it is always possible that such a book will come to your hand as Selzer came to mine. A book that cups your face in its hands and looks at you softly, eye to eye, at human distance.

Selzer, surgeon-turned-writer, frames this collection of essays as a one-way correspondence addressed to a novice of whom the writer is very fond. The tone is intimate, and the letters are about intimacy—the relationship of surgeon to his patient: to Selzer, a matter of awe. "The body," he says, "is the spirit thickened."

It is about the instruments of surgery, and the body itself—gallstones and wens and wounds and tumors—its beauty and ugliness—but more than that, anything about the human bond between the doctor and the wounded patient, a relationship Selzer understands as holy. The Latinate language of medicine is precise and rich. He loves the book and the word. Though he never gives explicit advice about writing, he might as well have titled the collection *Letters to a Young Writer and Editor.* Read *Letters* and test his prescriptions by substituting yourself—as reader, writer, or editor—for "surgeon" or "doctor." Think of the body of the work you're making or reading or editing as the physical body. "[A] physical examination affords the opportunity to touch your patient. It gives the patient to be touched by you. In this exchange, messages are sent from one to the other." It is a book about reciprocal bonds and responsibility: about compassion. Editors, I think, should have to take the Hippocratic oath: First, do no harm.

Any reader/writer (our left and right of the same human animal, aspects we can't separate "any more than you can separate a person's body from his spirit") is likely to find something of use in these essays; the lessons, being metaphoric, are wonderfully portable. He'll help you keep in mind that revision and editing of your own and others' work requires listening, as, diagnosing, a good doctor puts her ear to a patient's chest. The body of such work—often wounded—is as vulnerable as any naked patient exposed to the knife. The book can realign you, ease and open the jammed spaces between your joints to keep you flexible, adjust your mental posture, and moderate your textual rigidities. To consider the kind of reader and writer and editor, the kind of human being you want to be, "Listen to the patient," Selzer says, quoting Sir William Osler. "He is trying to tell you what is the matter with him."

I don't promise that Selzer will love you, too. Or heal you, or take out your gallstones, or clip your ingrown toenails, or sew up your wounds. He might help you heal your sentences. But he *will* help you think about how to be the kind of human being, reader, writer, and editor you want to be.

◣ ◣ ◣

Letters to a Young Doctor was originally given to me by David. At one time, as one of the few people among my friends who had a stable address, I had run something like a depression-era boarding house: if you were cold or hungry or just at loose ends, you could use the shower, get a bowl of chili, and crash on the couch for a couple of days. When I got off my waitress job at 3 a.m., friends and bar regulars and whoever they picked up would drift in: late-shift GM guys, fry cooks, demobbed vets and poets, and one out-of-work physicist—whoever had just drifted into town or was between one place and an as-yet-to-be determined somewhere else. When I got up early to take my four-year-old son, John, to Head Start, we'd skirt whoever was passed out on the living room floor. Some were good friends, some were more or less reliable, and since my son was fine company—my friend Bob called him the best argument he had ever seen for reproduction—there was always some-one around to read to him or pick him up when I had to work an extra shift. It seemed to me at the time that this motley, jury-rigged almost-family was a better-than-even trade for all the confusion.

It was a shaky, out of balance life, but John could sleep through anything, and since I'd been a reader all my life, I could always use a book to construct a quiet space, even with "Start Me Up" blasting on the stereo and drunks and dopers in the living room screaming over what punishment was too good for Richard Nixon. My focus on the page was so complete you'd have to set my hair on fire to make me look up. *A Canticle for Leibowitz* or *Varieties of Religious Experience* would soothe and fortify my psyche and maintain me at a more or less steady state—a daily shot of insulin to smooth out potential spikes or dips in my mental blood sugar. *In extremis,* I could always rely on bibliotherapy. I learned early that while discovering breadfruit with the Swiss Family Robinson, I wouldn't even notice when my father disappeared. Thick, rich books with lots of mental furniture and long, complicatedly subordinated sentences were a sure prophylaxis—accumulating forward motion, action continuing to rise no matter how many meaty nooks of digres-sion, until the turn when they pushed toward the promise of epiphany or resolution. From this solid base, I cultivated a subtler pharmacopeia, using books as boosters that dialed up moods as deliberately calibrated as any setting on Philip K. Dick's Penfield mood organ: Joyce Carol Oates's *Garden of Earthly Delights* for "melancholy anxiety under-laid with unarticulated ter-ror," or Jung for a "heighted sense of inner significance."

David—no known last name—came by occasionally. David was a regu-lar pacer of the streets, and Bob took him up when he found out David had an almost perfect memory for text and had read all the books Bob wanted to talk about but was too indolent to have finished. David was not easy company. He'd been diagnosed as schizophrenic and was spottily medicated with Ste-lazine. Silent, he could be a menacing presence, never making eye contact, always blocking the doorway you wanted to get through. But in his sweet spot, some snatch of drunken conversation would trigger him, and he'd pace with a ropey stride, firing off passages from Wittgenstein and Thomas Aqui-nas or verses from Lao Tzu in relation to the Gaia hypothesis, occasionally cutting so deep through the drunken bullshit talk that it started to bleed real blood. He brought to mind the philosopher who, on learning in kindergarten that English words were made up of the same 26 letters, immediately began trying to find a word that included the 27th. Though I could not get on his train of thought, he made my brain warble in a tingly, excited way, sparking arcs between synapses that had never before been in contact: promising that the grand theory of everything would make itself known if only all the right contacts lit up at once.

In an act of reciprocity that touched me—I had not imagined that anyone in his mental state would think of "hostess gifts"—David began to bring us books. The first was a boxed set of Lewis Thomas's *Lives of a Cell* and *The Medusa and the Snail*—and he brought one whenever he showed up, always science or natural history. (When functional, David worked at a distribution warehouse, and I later figured he'd lifted them off a loading dock.)

I read like David talked—profligate, uncensored. Early on, from the time I noticed that the cloud-shaped cartoon balloons that signaled thought instead of speech were connected to their characters' heads with bubbles and that the bubbles had spaces in between, I'd seen that reading was about open space as well as words, and that the trick of it was vaulting over them. As long as you could pick up even a few real snails in even the most foreign imaginary garden, you could make huge leaps over unknown meanings. At seven or so, reading *A Thousand and One Nights*, I learned that I did not need to know anything about caliphs or cuckoldry to reach the magic lamp. Then, every gap called out to me—first, inside one book, then among and between them—the fatter, the longer the sentences, the more impenetrable the vocabulary, the better. I was called to spin all the sentences I read together. They kept me leaning forward, grabbing at the thinnest strand of thoughts. If I could only make the right kind of sentences—long and long and longer, thickly embedded, double- and triple-jointed—I could braid together even the most tenuous, wispy threads.

I wrote sprawly, long-lined, ranty, momentum-fueled poems, one or two sentences to a page—and started to read them, touched up but unedited, at pick-up street corner readings. I inscribed my dreams on onionskin. Everything was thrilling, and synchronistic, and highly tuned. I had antennae everywhere, even on the soles of my tired feet, and my books were Dancing Wu Lee Masters. Nothing was separate, all was one, and I was one whole reading, writing, dervishing self. No matter how incomplete the rope of meaning I was trying to follow or to make, I could rely on it to take me, hand over hand, through any blizzard of bills or fog of anxiety.

Eventually, the chaos, as it inevitably does, turned to bedlam, and I began to clear the house. But even after Bob moved on and the crowd had petered out, David occasionally stopped by for a ride to the clinic or something to eat, and always left a book. Among them was *Letters to a Young Doctor*.

◄ ◄ ◄

I didn't read *Letters to a Young Doctor* until years later. We'd long moved across town without giving out our forwarding address. We no longer saw David striding by, arms swinging, head down, at the pace of traffic—and if I had, I would not have run out to ask him in. It was nice and quiet, John was in a decent school, I was much more highly degreed, and though I juggled jobs, I made an almost-living: temporary teaching, writing, editing.

I taught myself on the spot to do whatever paid, to juggle genres; I wrote brochures or advertising, and edited journal articles. As a line editor, I was hell on wheels, an expert surgeon: excise, slice, nip, shuffle, conjoin; transplant; fracture and set. I'd cut a sentence so tight it squeaked. Sometimes I couldn't stop, and—reading for pleasure or to tune a delicate mood—I'd take up a pencil, not to converse with the author or to copyedit, but to take up the slack in the sentence, or improve the assonance or euphony.

In my "real" work, I wrote a lot, and sometimes well. But I was still allergic to going idea- or purpose-first: when I knew too much, my sentences were flabby and the language turgid. Why write if I didn't amaze myself? So I developed a systematic regimen, always some aleatoric scheme that used a wild card or throw of the dice to set me off. Then I'd type as fast as I could, relying on velocity and the unconscious to outrun intention. For almost a year, I used *The Occult*, a gift from a missing friend, written by British autodidact Colin Wilson, not because I was so fascinated by Gurdjieff or ley lines, but because his language was so rich and dense. I'd roll a sheet into my IBM Selectric, flip the book open, stick my finger on a random phrase—"the nuns roared in strange voices," or "a slip set off an avalanche"—then riff on it. Twelve phrases, twelve sheets of onionskin, twelve riffs a day. Like the dreams I wrote, they'd go into a pile unread, to compost. When I eventually read them, some suggested a genre, an organic form; these I revised and published. But most of it was completely out of hand.

To get a lesson, I began to read for structure. I'd take my pencil and box up blocks of scene and exposition in books I admired to analyze the choreography. I was crazy to see how fine writing was made: the shape, the armature. I read like an X-ray machine, struck dumb by a brilliant skeleton. Ford Maddox Ford's *The Good Soldier*: impeccably balanced, as if each part had been weighed, letter by letter, on a gram scale, so assembled, the whole thing was stable on a fulcrum. What a feat! And Woolf's *The Waves*: prose with segmented parts that curved up and down like a long-necked monster, hinging itself through the seas. If I could have, which I couldn't, I'd have commandeered these shapes faster than David could pocket *Steal This Book*. I'd read backward from the shape itself into the hammer and tongs of it—how high the writer turned the heat, how she bent it over the anvil, and where she struck. But other than doing finger exercises, I could no more pattern my sentences after another writer's or drape a narrative over someone else's bones than I could levitate. I was incapable of taking any but the most metaphoric advice: Levertov's "organic form" or Gardner's "invisible dream in the reader's mind."

But in the months immediately before *Letters* finally came to hand, I could do none of this. I couldn't read or write at all. I felt as if I'd been trepanned with an entrenching tool. Sentences—written or read—were fractured, and my lifelong practices of bibliotherapy failed me, sure as god failed any whiskey priest. My eyes could pass over the page and extract words; my hands could make marks on paper, but it was all one word or phrase at a time. I had amnesia for the way the nouns stretched their hands toward verbs to make a clause, how one phrase or clause coupled with another to make a train of thought. I had forgotten how to let it draw me forward so meaning could accumulate, or bend back on itself. I could not see a sentence's "plot," let alone imagine that a string of them could follow on one another to make a "story." It was as if written language had been cleavered at the joints, and the parts scattered like the flesh and bones of dismembered Osiris.

The precipitating event was a public humiliation. The details are not so important except that without them, I would not have imprinted on *Letters to a Young Doctor*. Briefly: I was "invited"—pressed—to apply for a tenured job teaching writing in a residential science program, a position I would not have otherwise thought to apply for. Other than subscribing to *Science News* and editing a few science articles, I appeared to have few of the specific qualifications. But since the men who had invited me had read my work and knew what I offered, I could only suppose that they wanted a little poetic lightening up. Something like sending a poet up in space with the astronauts.

Even between working three jobs, I loved writing the job talk: finally the complex, flexing kind of piece I had imagined since the time I had started writing—one that balanced my centripetal and centrifugal urges, which so often confounded one another. It was not David's grand theory of everything, but it was as close as I could get. It was the time when first-person essays, with their various "I"s, were erupting everywhere, as if some pent-up force were breaking loose, so I anchored myself to Lewis Thomas's instructive and poetic essays in *Lives of a Cell*. It delighted me to see the mileage Thomas got out of "I wonder" or "I could not help but notice." I used feminist poetics—which I knew well—and ordinary language philosophy's speech act theory—which I had a crush on—to do the academic heavy-lifting. Suppose, I speculated, that instead of thinking of Lewis as a "popularizer," we interpret his work as a sign that scientific thinking had a pent-up need for speech acts only "I" could make, mental gestures that the evacuated prose of scientific articles repressed. Might these ways of speaking have family resemblance to revelatory, upstart, feminist poetry? A thought experiment, rephrasing Muriel Rukeyser: what would "split open" "if one [scientist] told the truth about her life?"

Everything I could get my hands on was in it: "I Stand Here Ironing," and Denise Levertov and William James and Lenore Candell ("I DEMAND AN ANSWER") and Stanley Cavell's *Must We Mean What We Say?* And the raven and the writing desk and the goddamned kitchen sink. The term "hybrid" was not used then, but it might have been called that: at once poetic and expository and plot-driven. And it was elegantly argued, too, if I did say so myself.

So when, in the interview after my talk, they went at me like Torquemada and his inquisitors, as if I had misrepresented myself as a biophysicist and they were going to interrogate me on the rack until I confessed and recanted, I was too stupefied to bite back or even curl in to protect my belly.

As with other such shames, the greatest humiliation was that I was too stupid to fight back at the moment, and so tried to armor myself after the fact.

I leaned in hard on the piece I'd written. If I could only perfect it, cure its flaws, I might perfect myself. I read it over and over, crazily perseverant, seeking out flaws or flaccid points or infelicities. I cut and cut and tightened until the words moaned, contracting so that there were no openings through which I could be attacked. I edited closer and closer, almost microscopically. Sometimes I would put my face right against the paper and squint at the shapes of the letters so that their limbs and serifs poked at me like briars and closed up over my head. I was exchanging molecules with the ink. By the time I realized that it had nothing to do with me—they'd already picked someone else and needed me to make a fool of myself so they could justify getting rid of me—I'd been so shamed, in my brain, in the spirit of my sentences, that I could not read or write. I'd edited myself down to nothing. It didn't happen all at once but over a few weeks; my senses began to fade out, as they do when you faint, the darkness and sound closing in on each side in cone-shaped shadows. You can see your vision narrowing, and then you go, without time to sit before you topple. It was as if letters in proximity to one another froze, as if made of Vonnegut's "ice nine" that froze everything it touched. I felt contagious, almost afraid to touch my son in case he'd freeze up. And I froze, too.

I'd taken my share of hits and knew depression well enough, but relied on my wit and native resilience to bounce back. I'd never before been in a state I could not at least ameliorate with text. But since I could no longer follow or construct a narrative, I could not medicate myself with reading and writing. The state I was in—it wasn't depression—it was thinkier and had a harder edge. I could not etherize myself with even the most primitive reading sedation, a self-comforting gesture that had little to do with meaning: it was the equivalent of thumb sucking, or perseverant back-and-forth rocking, each time gently bumping my forehead against the wall.

The previously infallible nostrum: I'd stack 1950s garage-sale mysteries next to the sofa in a pile like one of those faux-book sidetables you see in the airline shopping catalogs. The books were more or less indistinguishable, except that the ones discarded from libraries had plastic covers with pokey edges: an inch thick, light enough to hold overhead, even in hard cover, while I stayed horizontal. One murder to a book, no serial killings or subplots, a small cast of characters. Maybe a closed room mystery in which the fatal instrument turns out to be an icicle, or one in which the vicar did it. Nothing as literary as Ross Macdonald or George Simenon. I'd lie on the couch, chain-smoking the books like I chain-smoked Camels, outrunning misery with momentum, grabbing a sentence here, a sentence there, just catching enough to imagine I was getting the plot. As long as my eyes kept passing over text, whether I remembered from one paragraph to another who the protagonist was—naturally, at the pace of five or six a day, I got them mixed up—I could be some kind of okay. But unable to follow a sentence, even this was useless.

❧ ❧ ❧

I'd be lying if I said I remembered the exact moment that I picked up Selzer, that it was sitting on the kitchen table, that I turned to a certain page and saw a specific phrase, then a sentence, that it struck me on the forehead and threw me backward, healed as any damaged woman struck by a preacher at a tent revival. Maybe I was unpacking boxes, maybe it fell off an overcrowded bookshelf. Or maybe I saw the word "doctor." What did I read first? "Place your hand over your patient's heart"? "Cradle and steady him"? "The body is the spirit thickened"?

What I do know is that it came to hand, and that I opened it and heard it speak in a voice that "could induce sleep in a febrile insomniac." That Selzer took my face in both of his hands and held me, I-Thou. His prose wrapped around my body, and I felt it sigh and begin to warm and loosen. "I have depended," he tells the young doctor to whom the letters are addressed,

> upon the kindness of warm compresses. I suspect that wet heat applied to human flesh has done more to ease the plight of the sick than all the surgery past and all that is to come. A compress gives such insinuating warmth. It cooks the tissues gently, giving off a humid aroma, softening resistant fires, drawing out poisons, polishing and smoothing all the touch places of the body. . . . Anyone knows that to rekindle a near-cold fire, you place one faintly glowing ember against another, fan it for a moment, then sit back and watch a pretty flame break.

"Kindness," "compresses," "insinuating warmth." I had known how constricted my sentences had been, but not how tight my joints, how much my body ached: I'd forgotten I had one. To Selzer, the body's ugly, damaged parts—a "fierce, hot protuberance," "howling nerves," "blood spreading on the pillow," all have their own "beauty and grace." Who cannot grow warm to someone who sees the twenty bones of the foot "laced together with tendon, each ray accompanied by its own nerve and artery," "hands . . . pink and warm, each fingernail . . . trimmed in a gentle curve," and the tissue in your healing wound as "new pink buds of granulation tissue"?

As I began to apply my own warm compresses, to let my body be a "nest in which the setting bird huddles," sentences began to open: I could feel their breath. Print began to flex and stretch—no longer a thorny patch of letters. As my own body became more supple, language took on the pulsing liquidity of something alive and moving, as "the torpid intestine shifts its slow coils." I began to read again, to be drawn along, noun to verb, clause to clause, all pumping and peristalsis.

If I had picked up the book earlier, I might have cast a skeptic's eye on Selzer's "you" of intimate address, but at the moment it came to hand, my body *knew* that these letters were personally addressed to me—the sensation you experience when you open the mailbox and find an envelope with the handwriting of someone whose absence is a rent in your life.

I began to read, and later write, more fully than I had in years and with a more generous spirit. *Letters* radiates a compassion that my thinky self had lost, long before my recent injury. (When pondering what speech acts "I" could make, why had I not thought of "I understand," or "I forgive," or "I love you"?) Any reader or writer could substitute him- or herself for "doctor." "Reading with writerly eyes"? It did not have to mean disembowelment any more than removing an appendix.

More than anything, the writer's lesson to be taken from Selzer is compassion as the controlling principle—compassion toward your own work and the work of others. To be a generous, willing, compassionate reader. Like a surgery patient, the text waiting to be edited is unclothed and vulnerable, and before you insert the pencil, you should "place your hand on [its] shoulder," to be a "protective spirit" that will "cradle and steady" as you work.

Selzer does not tell you how to read or write or edit any more than he gives the young surgeon directions on performing heart surgery, but helps us think and feel, reflect on who we want to be. I can no more take Selzer into bits than read him with the critic's steely gaze: each sentence is self-same, fractally imbued with the intelligence of a loved, long-practiced craft applied with mercy.

What guides our practice, more than anything, is how we offer the gifts of our attention.

> [E]ach of you who is full-grown must learn to exist in two states—Littleness and Bigness. In your Littleness, you descend for hours each day through a cleft in the body into a tiny space that is both your workshop and your temple. Your attention in Lilliput is total and undistracted. Every artery is a river to be forded or dammed, each organ a mountain to be skirted or moved.

He imagines a miniaturized surgeon, who "in times of difficulty . . . could be lowered whole into the abdomen. There, he could repair the works, then give three tugs on a rope. . . . Presto!" When, in the midst of editing or revising, you think you might be in too deep, remember, "do no harm," remember "presto." And tug on your rope.

> At last, the work being done, you ascend. You blink and look at the vast space peopled by giants and massive furniture. Take a deep breath . . . and you are Big.

How hard it is to adjust your depth of field: You can't sew up an incision and make of a fissure a healing wound if you have forgotten how to lay your hands on the skin. Between up and down there's always the moment of repair, and to do it, you have to refocus on a human scale, the body of it, the living thing. It's at the skin where the incision you make must be sewn up to become a healing wound. Because, as the patient is a living thing, so is, when viewed with mercy, a piece of work; after surgery, it must be aroused from sleep. Gently, easily. No matter how maimed or twisted, it is some human being's spirit trying to thicken.

To forget when to immerse, and when to emerge. What writer or editor has not forgotten when to lift her head? Have you not perseverated, "[o]b-sessive beyond all feeling," forgetting that a sentence needs its air, and all kinds of breathing spaces? Have you not poked and poked at an infected phrase until something bursts and the whole body of work goes septic? Have you never not known when to stop, to be the surgeon who, when his patient died, repaired the cleft palate on her corpse, because he could not stop trying to make her beautiful?

If, while Little, you are inattentive, you can remove the wrong organ: and like the gallstone, "glistening, fruited, shiny," that goes "drab and dull when cut away from the body," it will never be the same even if you could put it back. Or be so eager to leave a signature, to emulate the arrogant surgeon who, to leave his mark of his abdominal surgery, excised every patient's belly button.

We all have our natural failing. Mine is getting stuck—either too Big or too Little, not knowing when to quit. And to be too "impatient to wield a scalpel." "Many the spleen," Selzer observes, "outsized and therefore delicate, has been ruptured by the undue pressure of the examining hand."

And mercy: who hasn't, enamored of our own cleverness and eagerness to turn a phrase, mocked another's mistakes to show our expertise, like teachers who delight too much in making lists of students' infelicities? This mean-spiritedness, an attitude Selzer calls contagious and in which most of us sometimes indulge, to be as "[s]uperb technicians . . . with unassailable credentials," who treat their patients with "abuse" or "flippancy." These are constant temptations of academics and journal editors and book reviewers, those whose work is to judge: it's easy to confuse our own skill with superiority, as if we do not make enough mistakes ourselves. To sharpen our words to show our cleverness, as if they were not projectiles aimed at a living being's guts.

But mercy is not the same as laxity. "To raise a flap of skin, to trace a nerve to its place of confluence, to carry a tendon to its bony insertion. . . . They are simple, non-theoretical, workaday acts, which, if done again and again, will give rise to that profound sense of structure that is the birthplace of intuition."

And with your own work, when you've persisted in too much dissection, you need to walk away: You need to know when "only a month of vacation can save you." To let yourself and the body of work and, as a reader, the body of literature you're called upon to judge, heal up from surgery, and come fully back to life.

To know the time for silence, and to listen: "lay your palm upon the patient's chest such that your fingers contact him everywhere. Now tap your middle finger to the middle finger of your other hand. Listen . . . no, feel, it is something between listening and feeling that you do here." And thus "you learn the language of the craft: bruit, murmur, trill (thrill?), flutter, fibulation . . . simple nouns that will soon become infused with knowledge and inspiration."

There have been long periods since first reading Selzer when I did or could not write; then life is dull, and I'm diminished, but I've never again been in the grip of reader's lock. Some of what I learned from him is permanent: to read others' work willingly, and—no matter what must be extracted or grafted—to do it with a generous heart, to recognize and preserve the healthy tissue. Because as the patient is a living thing, so—when viewed with mercy—is a piece of writing.

The lessons that are hardest to take, and that I need the most, and for which I have to revisit Selzer over and over, apply to my own writing. A writer's natural temperament can be a chronic condition. I get so easily out of whack. I get stuck in Little and don't know when to quit line-editing. Or I go too Big, and quotes and drafts and bits swirl in my skull, and brain's cartoon helium-filled balloons shoot off past the stratosphere while everything else falls comatose to the bottom of the page. Then I need to turn to Selzer as I go to my osteopathic physician, Dr. Grimshaw, to treat my hip joint when it seizes up. He lays on his gentle, generous hands to open space so it can breathe and flex. My body is made this way, a little lopsided. It can never be cured, though it can be eased, even partly corrected with regular visits. But only if I pay attention, if I am not too busy with other things. Compassion begins inside, Selzer reminds us; only then can it radiate outward.

◥ ◥ ◥

On Wednesdays, while other doctors golfed, Selzer would "withdraw from the practice" and repair to the library. Many lonely folks took refuge there: an elderly widower Selzer called "Neckerchief"—he did not know him by proper name any more than I knew David's last one. When Selzer asked Neckerchief why he limped and winced, he said it was his toenails: he could not get at them: "The nail of each big toe . . . was [t]hick as a thumb and curved . . . [w]ith each step, the nail would scrape painfully against the ground and be pressed into the flesh." The following Wednesday, Selzer brought his instruments, and in the library bathroom, knelt down, and firmly but slowly trimmed them: nip and file. It took an hour for each big toe. I would like to think that David, by some extension of distant energies, knows he gave me a kind of healing he could not use himself, and that if he is still alive, someone is right now performing for him such a kindness.

In Conversation With Our Contemporaries

AMY BUTCHER

Patricia Vigderman, *Possibility: Essays Against Despair*

LOUISVILLE, KY: SARABANDE BOOKS, 2013. 184 PAGES, PAPER, $15.95.

n her recent collection *Possibility: Essays Against Despair,* released earlier this year from Sarabande Books, Patricia Vigderman pairs the unlikely with the unlikelier. Conversations and meditations on Marcel Proust, W. G. Sebald, George Eliot, and David Foster Wallace work simultaneously—and often seamlessly—with the abstract and deeply personal: a consideration of Japanese art, a town in southwestern Texas, the hit film *Vertigo,* photography, and even depression. The collection is "like attending an ideal dinner party," Mona Simpson writes astutely, "where everyone has read your favorite books," but perhaps even more than that, one where the guests are the authors themselves, and they've very happy to oblige.

An experienced and talented writer in her own right—Vigderman's earlier work includes *The Memory Palace of Isabella Stewart Gardner* (2007), and she is a recent recipient of a Literature Fellowship from the Liguria Center for the Arts and Humanities—Vigderman's collection remains startlingly green, as yet untainted by cynicism or recent lofty conversations on navel-gazing. Instead, Vigderman's prose insists upon art as she prefers it, indeed, as many of us often employ it: as a mechanism for understanding the self or the reality we find ourselves in. Beautiful things, Vigderman seems to argue, are made more beautiful upon application.

As a whole, the collection brings to mind a discussion on New York photographer Richard Renaldi, whose latest work—"Touching Strangers"—pairs unlikely residents of New York City in roles that bespeak familiarity: siblings, lovers, neighbors, an elderly woman and her only grandson. Renaldi began the project six years ago and to date has collected hundreds of unlikely and intimate portraits whose sentiments—for both the viewer and the subject—strike a remarkably authentic tone. What proves most interesting about Renaldi's work is his capacity to forge an authentic sentiment from absolute inauthenticity, for while Renaldi is responsible for posing his subjects, he is in no way imparting any interior feeling. The subjects bring that themselves. Reports one subject, "I felt like I cared for her, like it broke down a lot of barriers."

Said another, "It was nice to feel that comfort."

But perhaps the most thought-provoking comment of all came from a middle-age woman, whom Renaldi paired with two young, blond teens, both of them in short-shorts and cowboy boots, leaning idyllically into her frame. "We're probably missing so much," she said, "about the people all around us."

Most photographers are known for capturing existence as it is, yet Renaldi has tapped into something more elusory, more enigmatic: he is capturing humanity for what it might be, indeed, what many of us wish it would be. And isn't it curious how seemingly easily?

My reason for mentioning Renaldi is two-fold: beyond feeling allowed—indeed, invited—to use another artist's work to further inform and explore my own, Renaldi's work seems founded upon the same main principle I perceive in Vigderman's collection. For while on the surface, *Possibility: Essays Against Despair* may seem a myriad of conversations about art and life, the collection appears instead to be a meta-observation on human thought: repeated moments of inspiration she finds as a conscious observer, listener, and reader, and she translates that energy into her prose.

On more than one occasion, Vigderman cites a trait she loves most about an artist, then attempts to master it on the page. In describing her experience reading Sebald's *Austerlitz,* for example, she writes, "I find I am reading it very slowly, almost word by word, following its winding sentences and paragraphs, and looking at its strange photographs . . . and sometimes going back and rereading pages or looking at how many pages are necessary for one paragraph (twenty-five is not unusual). I would say the effect is dream-like, entrancing, except that the associativeness, the quiet shifts and turnings, are also keeping me alert."

So, too, are Vigderman's, for this is precisely my reading experience. Like so many great writers whose voices are shaped by their contemporaries, Vigderman seems to try on styles as if shoes, allowing each one to ease effortlessly into her prose throughout the duration of her collection. At times calling to mind the prose stylings of David Foster Wallace, Proust himself, and occasionally Lydia Davis—whose "The End Of The Story" has long served as my own foundation in complicated simplicity—Vigderman's voice adapts to her material, and she moves as fluidly through language as she does through different kinds of subject matter. How else to describe "Eye Shadows," a three-page essay in which Vigderman moves first from Japanese art to architecture to used eye shadow sold on eBay? Like Sebald, Vigderman's essays explore the "possible co-existence of all moments of time in the space."

But this coexistence, of course, can prove problematic. In discussing writers whose work moves in narrative asides rather than arcs—Proust and James Joyce chief among them—Vigderman confesses that digression can often "lead both off the track and somewhere very interesting, depending upon your tolerance for lyric and syntactical uncertainty." Tolerance for the lyric: this seems exactly what Vigderman's collection aims to establish. How, then, can a reader remain engaged if the form itself mimics digression, a deviation, a departure?

Through the personal, it seems. Like the majority of writers and readers who've already reviewed Vigderman's collection, despite its relatively recent release, I found myself most sustained and indeed engaged with "My Depressed Person (A Monologue)," which appears at the very center of the collection. In it, Vigderman considers the near-crippling effects of depression, the complex nature of the "mind-body problem," and her own friendship with a person afflicted by this problem via David Foster Wallace's "The Depressed Person," whose own struggles—and ultimate submission—often assume the forefront of his work. "The terrible gift of David Foster Wallace's story," she writes, is "his knowledge of what it is to be lost of the grace of compassion."

"My Depressed Person" is engaging precisely for this reason: it is uncomplicated, straightforward prose on the profound subtleties of one's discontent. The depressed person, she writes, "is at the bottom of a well and all she can see hear touch feel taste smell is herself." What's more, depression is an enactment of "intense mercilessness . . . shame, the sense of being demeaned, the conviction that no one else has ever suffered comparably, the inability to describe the actual pain, and the isolation."

In short, I find the essay brilliant, not only for its argument, but because the prose itself functions so efficiently. The essay's close—with Vigderman and her depressed friend walking through a meadow—suggests *possibility*, which is essentially unavailable to the depressed and therefore informs the collection's title: to save oneself from despair, of course, one *must* believe in future prospects.

It's evident Vigderman has crafted art from an assortment of literary musings. Hers is a collection that is both thematically and formalistically interesting, and for me, it calls to mind the very beautiful articulation of Vigderman's own experience reading Sebald, which she describes in her essay, "Sebald in Starbucks":

> Loss of family, of country, or mind share in his sentences an unsensational space with sunlight coming through the feathers of a bird's wing, or a perfectly appointed billiards room left shuttered and untouched for a hundred and fifty years.

An unsensational space with sunlight coming through the feathers of a bird's wings—how unfamiliar, yes, but *true*.

Seeing Orange

A L E X I S   P A I G E

Piper Kerman, *Orange Is the New Black: My Year in a Women's Prison*

NEW YORK: SPIEGEL & GRAU, 2010; PAPER REPRINT, 2011. 327 PAGES, PAPER, $16.00.

Orange Is the New Black (a Netflix original series)

CREATED BY JENJI KOHAN; EXECUTIVE PRODUCERS JENJI KOHAN AND LIZ FRIEDMAN, PRODUCTION COMPANY, LIONSGATE TELEVISION; RUN TIME: JULY 11, 2013–PRESENT.

f one more person tells me that I *must* watch or read *Orange Is the New Black*, I fear my guts will explode. All summer people raved about both the hit Netflix series, created by *Weeds's* Jenji Kohan, and the 2011 best-selling memoir by Piper Kerman. Those recommending the show insisted it was addictive, authentic, nuanced, and ironic; to wit, the black transsexual character, the black lesbian character "Crazy Eyes," and the white, privileged main character used as "trojan horse." Critics called it fresh, pulpy, and political but with a light touch, because god forbid you are political with any heft.

In one telling review in *The New Yorker*, Emily Nussbaum writes,

> But while the show touches on the grinding unfairness of the penal system, it's never preachy or grim. It's very different, in other words, from the Sundance series "Rectify" (which just completed its run), a more delicate prison-themed series that relied on poetry and philosophy. "Orange" embraces a pulpier approach . . .

The assumption that one should never be "preachy or grim" gives me pause.

But of course there is a deeper reason for my resistance: I have been to jail. I spent 749 days in the Texas criminal justice system following a 2005 arrest for felony drunk driving. Drunk on red wine, I ran a red light and crashed into three other cars at a busy Houston intersection. A woman in one of the other cars broke her leg and underwent multiple nightmarish surgeries three days before her wedding. It was wrenching to have caused someone that kind of pain, and to imagine it could have been worse. As it was, it was life-changing.

Life-changing because I saw injustice firsthand, though I don't mean that my particular situation or outcome was unjust. On the contrary, my ultimate conviction of a lesser-included misdemeanor and 60 days in jail seemed exceedingly fair. But the experience gave me a window into the rampant racial disparities and the senselessness of drug enforcement that exist everywhere. The sum total of that experience, including two years of pretrial supervision and a five-day jury trial, left an imprint on me that would change the course of my life and leave me with the tattoo of incarceration.

At 2 a.m. on Easter Sunday in 2007, I was released from one of the largest and most fearsome county jail systems in the country, a place the U.S. Department of Justice has investigated for civil rights violations, including inhumane conditions and poor medical and mental health treatment, and which the DOJ and Harris County Sheriff's office have investigated for sexual abuse. That Sunday I was dumped along with 30 or so other inmates onto a downtown Houston loading dock at a witching hour and left there, put out like trash.

Unlike many other inmates deposited into the eerie predawn wasteland of the country's fourth largest city, I had people waiting for me—my brother and my now-husband—with a warm coat, a warm car, and cigarettes. Perhaps it is both a cliché and no surprise that I am white and most of my fellow released inmates were black, brown, or what was called "hillbilly white" in jail.

Though I lived in the Third Ward, a historically black and working-class neighborhood and the same from which many of these women hailed, we would return to our largely separate worlds—I to a life of privilege and they to another America. With only a misdemeanor conviction (secured by way of competent, expensive lawyers), a college education, employment opportunities (including employers who supported me through incarceration), and an opportunity to start fresh elsewhere, the world remained my oyster. If anything, I had taken a detour for some street cred.

During the years following my release, I grew troubled by many aspects of the criminal justice system as rendered in the American imagination—about pop culture representations of so-called criminals, the mentally ill, the poor, drug addicts and petty dealers, and of course people of color, who make up less than 30 percent of the population, yet more than 60 percent of those incarcerated. As Angela Davis shows in her book *Are Prisons Obsolete?*, the dominant American culture tends to view the penal system as natural, inevitable, and intractable: "At bottom, there is one fundamental question: Why do we take prison for granted?"

I had grown troubled, too, by the ways in which crime procedurals like my once-beloved *Law and Order*, reality shows like *The First 48*, *Scared Straight*, *The Big House*, or *Lockup*, not to mention more sophisticated shows like *Oz*, make people believe they understand the legal system and prisons, when in fact the real thing, in a telling paradox, remains hidden. I worry about these shows because as with anything else that hangs around the living room for too long—old catalogs, dog hair, and coffee cups—we become inured to them, anesthetized, and seduced by their ever-presence. You don't need to tell me about prison or the system, we think, I know about all that. But do we?

People pushed *Orange Is the New Black* on me because I am writing a memoir about my own experience in jail. Without being conscious of it at first, I set out to portray the utter strangeness of jail, to get behind that veil of clichés that stands in for the system, and I probably didn't want to believe that Piper Kerman could have done that, could have gotten there first. Of course it is ambitious to set out on such revisions of a collective imagination, maybe even glib to announce that as your intention, but if my goal is in part to get readers to revise their assumptions about prison, then I need to emphasize its strangeness and make it somehow not "the most obvious thing in the world," to borrow a phrase from Bertolt Brecht.

I did finally read *Orange Is the New Black*, and while I have some criticisms of it, the book didn't trouble me as much as the TV series and the praise the series has received. First, the memoir doesn't contribute to the onslaught of prison images, and second, while Kerman has a funny and ironic voice, the book rarely felt cheeky or flip. Both the show and the book choose narrative largely at the expense of social commentary. While I understand that telling a good story may be primary, I began to buck against the assumption that art/entertainment should not be too political or overtly political. This assumption is ideology cloaked as non-ideology, and it's one that activist writers confront every time someone accuses them of being political rather than artistic.

Certainly examples exist in literature and pop culture that challenge these assumptions, examples in which master storytellers have also exposed the reality of prison life: Ted Conover's immersion journalism *New Jack: Guarding Sing Sing*; Jimmy Santiago Baca's memoir, *A Place to Stand*; and *The Wire* and *The Corner*, two television series written by David Simon. In these examples, the stories are gripping, and the analysis of poverty, political corruption, our skewed and futile war on drugs, and the racism that drives our criminal system is unsparing.

One of the ways in which the collective delusion persists that prison is both a place we understand and yet one that remains special or unique is to explore it only through the lens of whiteness and/or economic privilege. "What was it like?" my white friends and family asked of jail. It's a question my bunkie Yolanda's friends and family likely didn't ask when she returned home to the Fifth Ward. They didn't need to ask because they lived in another America that is hidden from most whites, one where there is an institutional pipeline between ghettoized communities and the prison system.

Kerman often universalizes her whiteness, even as she acknowledges the racial reality of incarcerated life—from segregation to street rules. In some places, her awareness of this limited prism is keen, but in others she barely questions her own point of view or fails to see it altogether. Of course, she can't change the fact of her own whiteness or privilege, but what she fails to do too often is to examine when her own lens might be faulty, skewed, or privileged and then push herself to think about what the experience might be like for other inmates. She does give us their stories, but they come in snappy, well-written rap sheets—with just enough wit to acknowledge her own privilege, or so she thinks.

In one example, she is beginning to stand out because of the books and mail she receives:

It had gotten to the point where I was embarrassed, and also it made me nervous; it was a clear demonstration that I "had it like that" on the outside, a network of people who had both a concern for me and the time and money to buy me books. So far no one had threatened me with anything more intimidating than a scowl or a harsh word, and no other prisoner had asked anything of me. Still, I was guarded against getting played, used, or targeted. I saw that some of the women had little or no resources from the outside to help make their prison life livable, and many of my fellow prisoners were seasoned hustlers. (89)

When it becomes clear that the would-be "hustler" simply wanted to talk and borrow a book, Kerman must confront her assumptions: "When I thought about how terrified I had been of Rochelle, and why, I felt like a complete jackass. . . . Ashamed, I resolved not to be a jackass again." But even here she fails to interrogate why she was "terrified," assuming apparently that we, her (white) readers, will know what she means. But do we? Does she? What racial stereotypes led her to assume that any close encounter with a black woman constitutes a threat?

Kerman also doesn't sufficiently question her own ways of seeing. For example, when she says, "I 'had it like that' on the outside, a network of people who had both a concern for me," there is an assumption that "concerned" people will behave toward their incarcerated family or friends in the way Kerman's white, privileged family and friends behave. She posits a singular definition for the word *concern*. She omits the possibility that people might show concern differently—by taking care of the inmates' bills, lives, and families back home; by *not* sending money or accepting calls, because money is tight and better invested at home, or even that refusal of contact could itself be a show of concern.

In the Netflix series, the representation of white privilege often swings into caricature. Naïve protagonist Piper Chapman, who whines about prison food, shrieks in the shower, and stumbles around with her mouth open in nearly every scene, is perhaps the biggest dipshit in the history of dipshits. I understand this take on the character sells, but personally I don't buy it and I can't root for her. Fortunately, Kerman's portrayal of herself and her naiveté is more reliable in the memoir.

Another curious thread running through both the book and the show is the assumption that Kerman and her fellow inmates were in this together. On the surface, it is true that jail is a great leveler—we sleep together, use the bathroom together, shower together, eat together, and abide more or less by the same rules and codes. However, in significant ways, my experience of jail differed from that of the poorer women, especially the poor women of color. I became increasingly aware that because of my misdemeanor conviction, short sentence, and the resources I had on the outside, it would be easy for me to never return. This knowledge enabled me to maintain two versions of self—the inmate I had to be to survive jail, and the person I was outside of the context of this experience.

Additionally, the examples she chooses often seem offered as proof that she is not a racist. This she-doth-protest-too-much pose is wearying and disingenuous; the obsession with not wanting to seem a racist is whiteness writ large. The pathology of wanting to appear a certain way—kind, racially neutral, magnanimous, nonracist—paradoxically exposes the limits of her willingness to face the realities of racial difference. Look, for example, at this passage where she discusses her opportunity to move into a whiter, "quieter" dorm:

> B Dorm was certainly living up to its "Ghetto" moniker, with all the irritants of any ghetto [how would she know what all those irritants might be?]. One B Dorm practice alone drove me to the tooth-grinding brink of sanity: people would hang their little headphones on the metal bunks and blast their pocket radios through the makeshift "speakers," foisting their staticky music on everyone at top, tinny volume. It wasn't the music I objected to, it was the terrible audio quality. [Maybe, but she establishes musical tastes earlier, and they don't run toward rap, hip hop, R & B.]
>
> But A Dorm seemed populated by a disproportionate number of fussy old ladies [read white, even though they aren't tagged as such], plus the Puppy Program dogs and their people, who were mostly nuts. And I didn't want anyone to think I was a racist [okay, but why? What does this fear reveal?]— although nobody else in the Camp seemed to have the slightest compunction about expressing the broadest racial generalizations. [But not Piper who is almost pathologically polite, no matter what she might actually think.]

"Honey," another prisoner drawled to me, "everyone here is just trying to live up to the worst cultural stereotype possible." [Here is a perfect moment to interject something like, "perhaps that was true of me too."] (116–17)

Elsewhere, Kerman assumes that she, unlike others, confronts imprisonment the right way:

I saw that those who couldn't come to terms with their imprisonment had a very difficult time with staff and with other prisoners. They were in constant conflict because they couldn't reconcile themselves with their fellow prisoners. I saw young women who had been running wild in poverty most of their lives rail against authority, and middle-aged, middle-class women who were aghast to find themselves living among people they thought were beneath them. I thought they were all unnecessarily unhappy. I hated the control the prison exercised over my life, but the only way to fight it was in my own head. (138)

Here again she universalizes her own world view, her own rationality, and her own separateness. When she says she saw the others as "unnecessarily unhappy," what she fails to recognize is that for many of these women, their current circumstances were perhaps no better or worse than their "free world" circumstances; in other words, imprisonment was but one more expression of the worthlessness the world had always assigned to them. When she says "the only way to fight it was in my own head," she reveals her belief in self-reliance but fails to acknowledge that for others bucking the system may have been a rational way to "reconcile" incarceration, a way to have a little power in a world that had never given them any. I am sensitive to this blindness because I saw it in myself. As a middle-class white woman, I had always been rewarded by the world—by my parents, teachers, and even by the system itself—for maintaining a certain attitude. If I worked hard, smiled, and played by the rules, I could get along pretty well; the rules were made for people like me.

Finally, I think the book did what it set out to do, and I must acknowledge that some of my criticism grows out of my hopes for and anxieties about my own book. Overall, I enjoyed the memoir: Kerman renders well the drudgery of imprisonment, the friendships, the rituals, and she even confronts serious issues related to how prisons warehouse drug addicts and the mentally ill, and how so many women get caught up in the system because of racism and poverty, low-level drug involvement, and the sexual and physical abuse that makes them vulnerable to all of the above.

The show, on the other hand, is praised for confronting these issues with a "light touch," politically speaking. The aesthetic assumption that entertainment shouldn't be "too preachy or grim" is one forged by white privilege. We are supposed to want to be entertained—not to be moved. While we expect prison itself to be grim, we'd rather it be served pulpy in our living rooms—with just enough verisimilitude so that we can acknowledge the "grinding unfairness," congratulate ourselves for that acknowledgment, and continue to do nothing.

Yes, the Netflix series features an ensemble approach to characterization, a smart choice given the tendency in mainstream culture to defer to white voices. Yes, the characters are diverse in terms of race, class, and sexual orientation. Yes, a certain grit exists in the stylization of the show that makes it appealing, and yet while I understand that appeal, I am also troubled by it. Perhaps because I have been incarcerated myself, I am a little wary of manufactured authenticity, of the Hollywood tendency to add just enough "reality." I am wary of female inmates being reduced to punch lines and storylines and catch phrases. I am wary because I don't think these techniques really move us beyond voyeurism.

In the years since my own brush with the Texas criminal justice system, I have changed my mind about the role of art and entertainment on the subject; most art and entertainment (even the sophisticated stuff) simply rehash old myths that help maintain as "natural" a criminal justice system that incarcerates 2.3 million mostly black and brown and increasingly female citizens. I have come to believe we must look beyond the flood of supposedly reassuring images, images of a system just doing its job, images of CSI labs, courtrooms, squad rooms, militarized police tanks, Tasers, restraint chairs, holding cells, super-max facilities, crack heads, meth heads, and all manner of "others" held at a safe remove in what my Grandma Shirley used to call the "idiot box." The ubiquity of these images fosters a false sense of understanding and an indifference to the commonplace of injustice. Reality, John Berger argues, "lies beyond a screen of clichés."

I worry that our familiarity and comfort with certain prison images has made us inert. Why has there been no great outcry against the failed drug war, the mass incarceration, or the hideous racial and class disparities inherent in the system? Part of the reason, Davis argues, "has to do with the way we consume media images of the prison, even as the realities of imprisonment are hidden from almost all who have not had the misfortune of doing time." Shows like *Orange Is the New Black* let us think we're seeing prison when we're not. Such clichéd or manufactured images promote indifference to mass incarceration, and to what Michelle Alexander has dubbed "the new Jim Crow." As the jailingest society in the world, it is time for us to demand more of the images of prison that we're being offered. It is time for us to demand more of ourselves.

As They Lay Dying

S U Z A N N E   K O V E N

Katy Butler, *Knocking On Heaven's Door: The Path to a Better Way of Death*
NEW YORK: SCRIBNER, 2013. 336 PAGES, CLOTH, $25.00.

Meghan O'Rourke, *The Long Goodbye: A Memoir*
NEW YORK: RIVERHEAD, 2011; PAPER REPRINT, 2012. 320 PAGES, PAPER, $16.00.

Douglas Bauer, *What Happens Next: Matters of Life and Death*
IOWA CITY: UNIVERSITY OF IOWA PRESS, 2013. 168 PAGES, PAPER, $17.00.

Six weeks after his father died of a brain tumor, Philip Roth dreamt that the old man returned from the dead, furious that his son had buried him in a shroud. "I should have been dressed in a suit," the elder Roth scolded. "You did the wrong thing." When he awoke, Roth understood that his dream-father had been angered not by his son's choice of burial clothes, but by his writing of *Patrimony* (1991), the memoir in which Roth recounts the dream: "In the morning I realized that he had been alluding to this book which, in the unseemliness of my profession, I had been writing all through his illness and dying."

Roth is not the only writer who has taken notes at a parent's deathbed. Simone De Beauvoir's *A Very Easy Death* (1985) is a classic memoir about a parent dying, and the last several years have seen a boom in this sub-sub-genre: Blake Morison's *And When Did You Last See Your Father?* (1998),

Donald Antrim's *The Afterlife* (2007), Robin Romm's *The Mercy Papers* (2007), and Meghan O'Rourke's *The Long Goodbye* (2011) are but a few. This past year, two excellent books joined the growing list: Katy Butler's *Knocking On Heaven's Door: The Path to a Better Way of Death* and Douglas Bauer's *What Happens Next: Matters of Life and Death*.

When my own parents died—my father in 2004 and my mother in 2009—I felt a strong desire to write about them. Many needs fueled this desire: a need to make sense of my parents' lives and of my relationship with them; a need to expiate the tremendous guilt I felt in being unable to prevent their demise (the fact that I am a doctor compounded this guilt); and a need to face, on the page anyway, the inescapable message of my parents' declines and deaths, that my turn is next.

Surely people have always felt such emotions when losing their parents. So how to explain the rising numbers of memoirs about that experience just now?

Part of the explanation is the popularity of memoir generally, but the popularity of this particular kind of memoir reflects a demographic reality: people are living longer and dying more slowly than ever. Baby boomers, and the generations following them, are more likely to spend a prolonged period of time with dying, elderly parents than their ancestors did. During these months—or years—family conflicts intensify or resolve, long-hidden secrets are revealed, and parents and their adult children who have lived apart for decades may find themselves in newly intimate proximity. In other words, dying parents are good material for memoir. Or, to put it in less "unseemly" terms (to borrow from Roth), dying parents offer a memoirist an opportunity to tell a story that is both intensely personal and broadly resonant—i.e., what all memoirists hope to do.

Katy Butler's *Knocking on Heaven's Door* is both personal and resonant. Her account of the eight agonizing years between her father's stroke and his death is an ambitious hybrid of memoir, history, and self-help. She uses her family's unique circumstances as a springboard for a thoughtful discussion of why we subject people at the end of their lives to painful, expensive, and often futile medical treatments—and how we might avoid doing so.

In 2001, Butler's parents, Jeffrey and Valerie, seemed to be enjoying the perfect retirement. In their 70s they were both in excellent health and their home in Middletown, Connecticut, allowed easy access to the cultural and intellectual attractions of Wesleyan University, where Jeff had taught history. Their daughter Katy, a freelance journalist in her 50s then, lived in California. Her relationship with her parents had been conflicted at times and she was, as she writes, "comfortable loving [them] from a distance."

On November 13 of that year, Jeff suffered a stroke, the devastating effects of which his daughter describes this way: "The man who taught me how to take a bath would never again take one on his own. The man who taught me to revel in words and stories could not speak."

Butler's self-reference is not to be mistaken for self-pity or self-indulgence. She is making the point, as she does throughout the book, that illness affects not only the ill but a whole family. In the aftermath of her father's stroke, Butler became a member of the "roll-aboard generation," traveling back and forth across the country—her brothers absented themselves—to help her exhausted and often irascible mother care for her father. As she did, though, she was never quite certain of her proper role:

> A generation or two earlier, my path would have been clearly marked. I'd
> have moved into my parents' house, eaten the food at their table, and taken
> up the ancient burden of unpaid female altruism.

A year after Jeffrey Butler's stroke, his cardiologist recommended that a pacemaker be implanted in his chest to regulate a slow heart rate. The Butlers weren't sure that this intervention was a good idea for Jeffrey, who was, at that point, quite debilitated. But the cardiologist expressed no doubt about the device's benefit, so they agreed to it. "They had been," Butler writes of her parents, "by and large, in control of their lives and they did not expect to lose control of their deaths." And yet, lose control they did. For seven years, the pacemaker "kept [Jeffrey's] heart going while doing nothing to prevent his slide into dementia, incontinence, near-muteness, misery, and helplessness." A year before Jeffrey died, Valerie asked her daughter's assistance in having the pacemaker turned off, in effect euthanizing Jeffrey. Katy Butler agonized over making this request, which, it turned out, no doctor would honor.

Knocking on Heaven's Door is a rich and detailed portrait of one family. We learn of Jeffrey and Valerie Butler's courtship in their native South Africa, Jeffrey's loss of an arm in World War II, Katy's happy childhood in Oxford, where her father finished his graduate studies, and her less happy adolescence and young adulthood in the United States. Katy's descriptions of relationships with her parents, her brothers, and the lover she leaves behind in California with each trip east are dynamic and multidimensional. At times, for example, her mother's nagging and criticism infuriate Butler so much that she severs contact with her; at other times, Butler sees fellow Buddhist Valerie as her "dharma sister." One senses that these conflicting feelings often coexist.

Unique as Butler's family's story is, she emphasizes that because we live in a society that hasn't figured out how to implement medical advances wisely, or how to allow people to die in a dignified way, many other families are having similar experiences. As Butler puts it,

> Every day across the country, family caregivers find themselves pondering a medical procedure that may save the life—or prevent the dying—of someone beloved and grown frail . . . This is not a burden often carried by earlier generations . . . We are in a labyrinth without a map.

At the end of *Knocking on Heaven's Door*, Butler offers "A Map Through the Labyrinth," practical advice on caring for elderly parents and making decisions about medical treatment at the end of life. She includes information about hospice and palliative care, dividing duties among siblings ("Don't let brothers off the hook"), and resisting a "never-say-die death in intensive care."

Butler also offers this piece of somewhat less-expected advice: write. During Jeffrey Butler's decline, Valerie kept a journal in which she recorded both her frustration with her husband and her shame at being frustrated. Jeffrey himself toiled over a brief autobiography of his wartime experiences. And Katy Butler exchanged "love letters" with her dying father:

> They were simple letters, as if written by a five-year-old girl. Knowing that his visual brain was less damaged than his language centers, I put drawings in the margins and within the text . . . I no longer had to worry about how he'd edit my work or what he'd say about my risky career. He wrote back more tenderly than he could speak. It was the laboring that counted for me, the fact that he'd spent an afternoon making something, a gift, for me.

Knocking On Heaven's Door, too, is a gift to readers—especially those who have cared for or will care for dying parents (i.e., most of us). Butler offers a map through the labyrinth of medical decision-making but, more importantly, through the emotional wilderness that a child of any age enters when a parent is dying.

◣ ◣ ◣

Meghan O'Rourke was barely in her 30s when her mother died of colon cancer. In *The Long Goodbye*, her memoir about losing her mother, O'Rourke, like Butler, rails against the aggressive last-ditch therapies that make the end of life so miserable for patients and their families. "Hell, I thought bitterly," she writes, with the sharp intelligence evident throughout her book, "[is] technology in the presence of inevitable death." O'Rourke doesn't gloss over the endless rounds of chemo, the frequent CAT scans, and emergency room visits that marked the degradation of her vibrant mother into a helpless and pathetic creature. But O'Rourke's subject is not so much dying as its aftermath: grief. For her, grief is the labyrinth with no map.

Grief disorients O'Rourke for both general and personal reasons. Generally, she argues, our society's skittishness about grief makes it difficult for those in mourning to heal, or even to articulate their pain:

> Although we have become more open about everything from incest to sex addiction, grief remains strangely taboo. In our culture of display, the sadness of death is largely silent. . . . What does it mean to grieve when we have so few rituals for observing and externalizing loss?

More personally, O'Rourke's grief is complicated by the fact that, unlike Katy Butler, she was quite young when her mother died. While the reversal of roles—child caring for parent—is difficult at any age, it's especially challenging when the child is still emotionally dependent on the parent. Barbara Kelly O'Rourke died at 55. The memory of her as the fun, cool mom who worked as a popular administrator at her kids' school was still fresh in her daughter's mind when she was called upon to bathe and feed her. "Was I still her child?" O'Rourke wonders poignantly. In an emotional tailspin as her mother was dying, O'Rourke rushed into marriage, divorced eight months later, and had an ill-advised affair. In other words, she was a young woman who really needed her mother. O'Rourke writes: "I was irrevocably aware that The Person Who Loved Me The Most In The World was about to be dead." This is a sentiment shared by "orphans" of any age—a 60-year-old friend whose mother died recently asked me, with a sad smile, if I would "adopt" her—but one senses that O'Rourke's orphanhood isn't the kind in quotation marks.

Compounding her grief is the fact that O'Rourke suffers from anxiety, particularly about death. As a child, her mother comforted O'Rourke when she confided her fear. And unexpectedly and movingly, caring for her dying mother also helps assuage her anxiety. Thinking about how she and her brothers needed to help her mother up from the toilet, she writes:

> It was what she had done for us, back before we became private and civilized about our bodies. In some ways I liked it. A level of anxiety about the body had been stripped away, and we were left with the simple reality: Here it was.

Like Butler, O'Rourke writes (and reads—*Hamlet*, C. S. Lewis) to make sense of her pain. At five, she had been encouraged by her mother, who gave her a red corduroy-covered journal. O'Rourke now writes, as she puts it, to "find a metaphor" for her mother's death. But she seems less confident than Butler about the healing power of writing. At the end of *The Long Goodbye,* fifteen months after her mother's death, O'Rourke admits that while she has committed her grief to the page by writing her memoir, and does feel somewhat better for having done so, that grief lives on:

> What can I say? There's nothing "fixed" about my grief. I don't have the same sense that I'm sinking into the ground with every step I take. But there aren't any "conclusions" I can come to, other than personal ones. The irony is, my restored calm is itself the delusion. I'm more at peace because that old false sense of the continuity of life has returned.

For Douglas Bauer, the "continuity of life" appears, at first, to be no comfort. In his memoir, *What Happens Next?*, Bauer moves back and forth between his mother's death and the series of infirmities that signal his own aging. An answer to the question he poses in the title of the book seems clear: *your parent dies—and then you do.*

What could have been a depressing theme becomes, in Bauer's skilled hands, a lyrical reverie. *What Happens Next?* includes nine loosely linked essays that, as Bauer advises in his introduction, can be read individually but are best "read from start to finish, since it's organized to move along with a sense of the tale gathering and building."

The "tale" is really two tales: Bauer's mother's story and his own. In his early 60s, Bauer underwent cataract surgery. The operation was, like Bauer's stiff knee and the rapid heartbeat he'd noticed on occasion, nothing serious. But, he writes of these minor afflictions, "[i]t was as if they'd colluded in a devilish partnership to simultaneously launch the beginning mischief of age." Bauer woke from surgery in Boston to learn that his mother had just died, at 86, at a hospital in his native Iowa. He'd initially pictured himself hooked up to an IV at the very moment his mother had been similarly connected. But having learned from his brother that, in fact, his mother had no IV when she died, he writes:

> So I had been mistaken. We had not been joined, my mother and I. We'd not
> been twinned in the moment. We'd not been allied, except as a contrivance,
> through the unseemly [Roth's word again!] ease of my imagination. I would
> need to think on our history, hard and patiently, before it could be more than
> heavy-handed metaphor to say that I'd begun to see the world clearly on the
> day, in the hour, my mother died.

This combination of narrative humility and curiosity suffuses Bauer's lovely essays. Time and again he picks up possibly related phenomena and rather than forcing them to serve as metaphors for one another, invites us to explore them side by side. In "Tenacity," he interweaves images of his own faithfully beating heart on echocardiogram with his mother's several-hour crawl to the telephone after she fell and broke her hip, with the men at the shelter where Bauer volunteers: "They lived, these men, dog years of illness and abuse: one year aged them seven." In "What We Hunger For," memories of Bauer's long friendship with M. F. K. Fisher, whom he interviewed for *Playboy* as a young writer in 1971, inevitably bring up memories of his mother's kitchens. And Bauer conflates Fisher's death with his mother's and, by implication, his own. The book's final lines are:

Mary Frances and my mother. The two of them in desperate unison, become
the same as they fought for life as life was leaving them; their gasping lungs;
their frantic hearts; fortunate to grow old, disintegrate, and finally die.

Bauer doesn't specifically prescribe writing as balm for the confusion and
pain of losing a parent, as Butler and O'Rourke do, but it is clear in *What
Happens Next?* that he believes it is. How else to explain the gratitude with
which he faces the prospect of his own eventual death at the end of the book?
Or the hope he leads his readers gently to share: that one day we may be as
"fortunate" to age and die as our parents did?

Good News for Nonfictionists

PATRICK MADDEN

Jill Talbot, ed., *Metawritings: Toward a Theory of Nonfiction*

IOWA CITY: UNIVERSITY OF IOWA PRESS, 2012. 217 PAGES, PAPER, $39.95.

B. J. Hollars, ed., *Blurring the Boundaries: Explorations to the Fringes of Nonfiction*

LINCOLN: UNIVERSITY OF NEBRASKA PRESS, 2013. 268 PAGES, PAPER, $30.

'll begin by making a few assumptions about you, dear reader, based on your subscription to or at least borrowing of *Fourth Genre*: you are high-minded. Your taste is excellent. You favor or are at least curious about creative nonfiction. Perhaps, feeling this phrase a bit presumptuous, you prefer a different term, such as "literary nonfiction," or you reach back to older genres, such as "memoir" or "essay." You may teach. You certainly learn. You likely write. You lament the degraded cultural moment when safe and formulaic art achieves the widest popularity and rakes in nearly all the money, when art in all its forms is widely seen as impractical, frivolous, unworthy of public backing or even consideration. You support the arts and feel that they are fundamental to your conception of the world. You wish more people shared your perspective because if they did, we would be kinder and more curious, more open to experience, and more willing to live and let live.

I have good news, I think. Although I'm not entirely sure how cultural evolution happens, whether teachers have the power to nudge students toward maturity and improvement or simply to reflect changes already afoot, I'm cheered by a number of new anthologies that suggest a fulfillment of Joseph Epstein's decades-old prophecy: "It's a sweet time to be an essayist" (for me, *essayist* encapsulates or supersedes all other names one might call a "writer of creative nonfiction"). If you're nonplussed by my extrapolation from *essayist* to the "hope for the world" reflected in my claims, then perhaps the books I recommend are not for you. But if you see/hope for the connection, then please read on.

Granted, I have not been alive long enough to witness first-hand long patterns of publishing, but I *have* been paying attention for the past dozen years or so, and I've consulted older, wiser friends who've been paying attention longer, and I believe that this recent slew of works focused on exploring and teaching the literary side of nonfiction is unprecedented. Although some older anthologies grace my library's shelves, they were published sparsely across the years, and they tend to be one or the other: collections of creative work or of criticism. However, 2012 and 2013 brought us a windfall of books that are right up our alley, combination creative-critical anthologies that teach and inspire by example *and* by analysis.

In this review, I focus on *Metawritings: Toward a Theory of Nonfiction*, edited by Jill Talbot, and *Blurring the Boundaries: Explorations to the Fringes of Nonfiction*, edited by B. J. Hollars. In the next issue, I'll complete my overview, covering *Understanding the Essay*, edited by Patricia Foster and Jeff Porter, and *Bending Genre: Essays on Creative Nonfiction*, edited by Margot Singer and Nicole Walker. Other books of this ilk have been reviewed previously or will be reviewed soon in these same pages. It is not in my nature, nor in the nature of a review such as this, to lambaste books, only to recommend them, and I do recommend these, wholeheartedly, but I will also try to set them apart one from another, to characterize them in descriptive ways that can reveal something of their content and guide would-be readers and course-adopters.

Both books follow a similar felicitous format, publishing recent creative work by contemporary luminaries in the field of creative nonfiction paired with commentary by the authors about their process or focus or writing decisions and strategies. In the case of *Metawritings*, the commentary comes in the form of a brief interview (often with long answers). In *Blurring the Boundaries*, the commentary is a short essay focused on an aspect of craft, such as point of view or research or humor. I've rarely seen this kind of self-criticism available and when I have, it was nearly always separate from an author's creative work (perhaps in a literary journal interview). *Fourth Genre*'s "Essays with Commentary" feature is a notable exception. So, these books perform a useful service in bringing them together, and then in bringing together a number of similarly patterned pairings. So each book practices what it preaches, joins together between the covers both example and instruction, or at least gives a peek behind the curtain of the authors' thinking about writing to demystify the process, to temper the naïve notion that "the muses made me do it"; inspiration, sure, but also study and adoption and intention and craft.

In *Metawritings*, for instance, you'll find original work by Ryan Van Meter, Brenda Miller, Kristen Iversen, Brian Oliu, and nearly a dozen other writers, all explicitly writing about writing (or writing in ways that call attention to the writtenness of the text) but not in imperative, instructional ways. Instead, there is Robin Hemley in Prague *trying* to get pickpocketed to learn a thief's story, and not only trying to get pickpocketed, but also telling readers about the process of deciding on the plan, despite friends' objections, and then failing to get pickpocketed but writing about the experience anyway. There's Sarah Blackman writing in third person, declaring the difficulty of her subject before launching into the fictions we project about ourselves. There's Bernard Cooper, thrilled that his book has won the Ernest Hemingway Award but worried that his father might now read the book, which portrays him unflatteringly. Editor Jill Talbot declares that the premise of *Metawritings* is to "turn a spotlight on metawriting in order to showcase the various ways in which it is currently being performed," and the book does this admirably, intriguingly. But it also demonstrates that metawriting has long been with us. As David Lazar says in his interview, "The essay is by its nature a self-reflective form, a form through which the self's prism considers the world. Montaigne's essays are full of the discourse of the essay, because in discussing the self, creating the self through which one essays the self, one essays one's essay."

Blurring the Boundaries, however, includes pieces by Ryan Van Meter, Robin Hemley, Brian Oliu . . . wait a minute! Actually, those are the only three writers repeated across the two books, and their essays are different in each. *Blurring the Boundaries* includes more than twenty writers and, even at a glance, their essays are often recognizably unconventional. Marcia Aldrich's "The Structure of Trouble" uses indentations, subheadings, white-space, questions, warnings, and even a word cloud to essay *trouble*, or perhaps to trouble *trouble*, especially through the lens of personal relationships with loved ones. Naomi Kimbell uses the form and voice of a scientific inquiry to dispute that those who witness "insubstantial phenomena" are "psychotic." Michael Martone begins with an asymmetrical photo of his face and then digresses into a narrow column of right-justified meditation on Bell's palsy (and much more). Ander Monson's well-known "Outline Toward a Theory of the Mine Versus the Mind and the Harvard Outline," written in outline form, makes an appearance, along with his outlined reflections on it. Dinty W. Moore shares direct "tips" for writers (in a sidelong, humorous way). Several authors break their pieces into brief fragments with only juxtaposition and friction to hold the whole and suggest meaning. Several authors discuss in their critical passages their decisions to utilize deliberate fictions to bolster their subtle nonfictional arguments. But the book's blurs aren't only across the fiction/nonfiction line. Eula Biss's "Time and Distance Overcome," for instance, grows from historical research into a kind of journalistic project. In her explanatory note after, she reveals an important lesson for writers: that she "was planning to write an essay about telephone poles and telephones, a subject [she] hoped to maneuver into a metaphor for collective efforts to stay in touch." She "was not planning to write an essay about lynchings." But as her research turned up article after article about Jim Crow vigilantism and racism, her essay found its subject, and its form, a litany, which "in its anaphora and repeated patterns and deliberate redundancy . . . create[s] a brutally repetitive experience for the reader." Again and again through the book, authors provide valuable insight into their process, illuminating the dark path to a successful and moving work of creative nonfiction.

As I read the essays and metaessays in these books, I felt spurred time and again to jot down a note toward an essay of my own, either a new work or an existing one that might be expanded and improved by the insight I gleaned.

And thus I expect that readers will appreciate that *Blurring the Boundaries* includes an added bonus for writers and teachers: a detailed writing exercise for/from each piece in the anthology. So, for instance, in response to Steven Church's "Thirty Minutes to the End: An Essay to My Aunt Judy on the Occasion of the May 4, 2007, Tornado" (the title of which sums up the essay nicely), B. J. Hollars invites readers to write about a distant event based on interviews with first-hand witnesses. For Kim Dana Kupperman's "71 Fragments for a Chronology of Possibility" (which refrains William Carlos Williams's "So much depends upon . . . "), Hollars recommends creating a set of fragments based on the numerical title of another work (for instance, "When I'm 64"), repeating a borrowed phrase from another favorite work (for instance, "No one perhaps has ever felt passionately towards . . . "). In most of the prompts, subject matter and theme (the easiest paths of imitation) are beside the point. We are to learn technique and form from these essays, and we are to be inspired by their art.

But even when the call to write is not explicit, these books inspire oblique imitation by simply collecting so much excellent writing in one place. In my opinion, both are well-suited to student-writers, which should include all of us, because they allow us to look under the hood and see the machinery that makes such moving creative nonfiction. It's no secret that voracious reading is prerequisite to writing well, and that gathering insight into the ways writers write eases the mechanical work of discovering how good writing succeeds, so the self-reflexive critical commentary is quite valuable as well.

You've made it this far, reader, so I feel I can trust you with a small caveat. I must admit a tinge of disappointment that so many of the theoretical constructs advanced in the books seem simply to suggest that injecting a little bit of fiction into a supposed nonfictional text is sufficient to bend genre or blur boundaries. This seems a rather naïve assumption, or at best a response to other naïve assumptions. Although Montaigne swore that "I have forbidden myself to dare to alter even the most light and indifferent circumstances; my conscience does not falsify one tittle," essayists and memoirists from then on have toyed with fictions in their supposed nonfictions, have seemed either not to care about any generic prohibitions or proscriptions, or have seen genre as a set of formal expectations inherent or discoverable in texts themselves, not in an extra-textual promise of fidelity to fact. So I don't think that *fiction/nonfiction* are interesting generic distinctions (as *story/essay* are), yet I recognize that this is the cultural moment we occupy in which nearly every Q&A after a nonfiction panel at the AWP conference includes a discussion of boundaries and acceptable breaches of the fictional into the nonfictional. So I don't fault these books for addressing the issue. And I'm pleased as punch that they're about so much more. They're good books, really good books. They speak well for and bolster the continued vibrancy of our art form.

ABOUT THE CONTRIBUTORS

Judith Adkins has an MFA in creative writing from George Mason University and lives in Alexandria, Virginia. Her work has appeared, or is forthcoming, in *Ruminate*, *The Colorado Review*, and *The Normal School*. She is at work on a collection of essays exploring gay and lesbian family matters.

Amy Butcher (amyebutcher.com) is a recent graduate of the University of Iowa's Nonfiction Writing Program and is a recent recipient of the Olive B. O'Connor Creative Writing Fellowship at Colgate University. Her essays have appeared in *The Paris Review, Tin House, Salon, The Kenyon Review, The Indiana Review, The Rumpus, Hobart*, and *Brevity*, among others.

Jill Christman's memoir, *Darkroom: A Family Exposure*, won the AWP Award Series in Creative Nonfiction in 2001 and was recently reissued in paperback by the University of Georgia Press. Her essays have appeared in *Barrelhouse, Brevity, Harpur Palate, Iron Horse Literary Review, Literary Mama, River Teeth*, and many other magazines and anthologies. She teaches creative nonfiction in Ashland University's low-residency MFA program and at Ball State University in Muncie, where she lives with her husband, writer Mark Neely, and their two children. More at jillchristman.com.

Kate Carroll de Gutes holds an MFA from the Rainier Writing Workshop. Her work has been published in various journals, including *Seattle Review, New Plains Journal, Crosscurrents*, and *Pank*. Kate lives in Portland, Oregon, where occasionally you might see her wearing a tie and chatting up some tall femme.

Robert Long Foreman is from Wheeling, West Virginia. He has won a Pushcart Prize, and his fiction and nonfiction have appeared in *The Cossack Review*, *Third Coast*, *Willow Springs*, and *AGNI*, among other journals. "Dirty Laundry" is included in his book-length work on inheritance, *We Are All Dealers in Used Furniture*, which is under submission to publishers. He teaches creative writing and literature at Rhode Island College.

Amanda Giracca lives in western Massachusetts, where she just completed what she believes to be her last season as a landscape gardener. Her essays and stories have appeared in *Flyway*, *Terrain.org*, *The Magazine*, and *Passages North* among others, and she is a regular contributor to *Vela Magazine*. She received an MFA from University of Pittsburgh and is currently a lecturer in University at Albany's Writing and Critical Inquiry program.

Michelle Pilar Hamill received her MFA in creative writing from Vermont College of Fine Arts in 2012. She won Honorary Mention at the AWP Intro Journal Awards. Her essays can be found on *Fresh Yarn*. She is currently working on her memoir, *Sparkle Head*, and lives in Manhattan with her husband, daughter, and two ex-alley cats.

Suzanne Koven (suzannekovenmd.com) practices primary care internal medicine in Boston. She writes the monthly "In Practice" column for the *Boston Globe* and blogs at *boston.com*. She also contributes the interview column, "The Big Idea," at *The Rumpus*. Her essays and reviews have appeared in *New Yorker.com*, *The New England Journal of Medicine*, *Psychology Today*, and other publications.

Patrick Madden teaches at Brigham Young University and Vermont College of Fine Arts. His first book, *Quotidiana*, won an Independent Publisher Book of the Year award, and his essays have been published widely in journals and anthologies. He is completing his second book, *Sublime Physick*, and an anthology with David Lazar, *After Montaigne: Contemporary Writers Cover the* Essays.

David Naimon is a writer and host of the literary radio show, Between The Covers (KBOO 90.7 FM), in Portland, Oregon. His work can be found in

Tin House, StoryQuarterly, ZYZZYVA, and *The Missouri Review,* among others.

Alexis Paige's work has appeared in *The Rumpus, Pithead Chapel, Ragazine, 14 Hills,* and on *Brevity*'s blog. Winner of the 2014 New Millennium Writings Nonfiction Prize, she also received a recent Pushcart Prize nomination and a feature on *Freshly Pressed* by WordPress. Twice named a top-ten finalist of *Glamour Magazine*'s essay contest, Paige holds an MA in poetry from San Francisco State University and is pursuing an MFA in nonfiction from the Stonecoast creative writing program.

Patricia Park teaches writing at CUNY Queens College. She graduated from Swarthmore College and received her MFA from Boston University. She has received writing fellowships with Fulbright, the Center for Fiction, and the American Association of University Women. Her essays have appeared in the *New York Times, the Guardian, Slice Magazine, Brevity,* and others. Her debut novel *Re Jane* is forthcoming with Penguin/Viking Books.

Pat Rathbone is a psychologist who taught at Harvard University and prac- ticed psychotherapy in the Boston area. She studied English at Smith College and Yale and has published short stories and completed a novel. Diagnosed with pancreatic cancer in 2008, she was for a time unable to write fiction, turning instead to explorations of her own situation. She is back at work on a second novel.

Leonora Smith writes poetry and prose and teaches at Michigan State Uni- versity in the Department of Writing, Rhetoric and American Cultures. She's published a book of poems, *Spatial Relations,* and several chapbooks, "Eating Red Meat," and "Faculty X" (based on randomly selected phrases from Colin Wilson's *The Occult*), and has published in literary magazines including *Exquisite Corpse, Alaska Quarterly Review, New Letters, Sin Fronteras, Intro, Nimrod,* and *Poems from the Third Coast.* She is currently working on a grand theory of everything.

Sheryl St. Germain's books include *How Heavy the Breath of God, The Jour- nals of Scheherazade,* and *Let It Be a Dark Roux: New and Selected Poems.* A memoir about growing up in Louisiana, *Swamp Songs: the Making of an Unruly Woman*, was published in 2003, and she coedited, with Margaret Whitford, *Between Song and Story: Essays for the Twenty-First Century*. Her most recent book is *Navigating Disaster: Sixteen Essays of Love and a Poem of Despair* (2012). She currently directs the MFA program in Creative Writing at Chatham University where she also teaches poetry and creative nonfiction.

Kathryn Winograd is a poet and essayist. Her poetry has won the Colorado Book Award, and her nonfiction has been published in numerous literary journals and magazines. She teaches poetry and creative nonfiction in the Ashland University MFA program.

Olivia Wolfgang-Smith holds a BA in creative writing from Hamilton College and is pursuing an MFA in fiction at Florida State University. Her writing has been named a finalist for *Glimmer Train*'s Short Story Award for New Writers, nominated for the Pushcart Prize, and published in *The Common* and elsewhere. She is originally from Rhode Island.

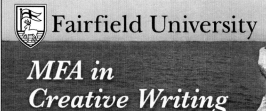

Fairfield University

MFA in Creative Writing

Low Residency Program

- 14 books published by alumni over the past two years
- Merit and need-based scholarships available
- New! Life after the MFA guidebook
- Post-grad teacher training program
- A spectacular coastal setting for residencies
- Concentrations in fiction, poetry, nonfiction and scriptwriting/playwriting
- Faculty mentoring by award-winning authors and poets
- Workshops with NYC editors and agents
- Study abroad residency programs in Galway and Florence

Program Director:
Michael White

RECENT GUEST WRITERS

Mark Doty
Carlos Eire
Mary Karr
Wally Lamb
Rick Moody
Philip Schultz
Anita Shreve
Sue William Silverman
Charles Simic

Published Alumni

"Without the support of other writers and feedback from experienced authors in Fairfield's MFA program, I wouldn't have obtained a book deal with Harper Collins."
- David Fitzpatrick, MFA '11
Author - *"Sharp"*

Inspire the writer within...

Summer 2014 Residency
July 18 - July 27

rest in peace man who, once upon a time and in order to make ends m̶
up the teaching of a class called "Public Speaking" at a Midwestern uni
ty whose main claims to fame included having a train engine for a masc
playing host to highly ranked engineering and agriculture programs, th
which had a lot to do with why the communications department had i̶
rule discouraging the bringing of animals or pets of any kind to class, si
had apparently been problems with students dragging hogs and calves a̶
ponies down flights of stairs and into classrooms where they (the anima̶
no doubt as scared shitless as the students whose charge it was to give a̶
consisting of little to no verbal filler and effortless transitions and next t
strange gestures, like the repeated rubbing of an eyebrow that one corn̶
head with a goatee had repeatedly engaged in during his speech, but th̶
was that one guy in the deceased's class had argued that his particular p̶
be okay to br̶ passagesnorth.com e whole time
as some specie̶s of Austra̶lia̶n flying squirrel whose name the deceased w̶
unable to remember, was only the size of a finger, so anyway the decea̶s
and the kid brought it in and the flying squirrel or whatever was terrific̶
would not for any reason let him or herself be pried with the kid's shak̶
____t of the kid's shirt pocket and so the kid went around to each
_____ending over to let those who were interested peek inside his
_____of course, awkward and not so effective, since the shadow o̶
_____d who was looking in often obscured the little guy or gal i̶
_____as indeed embarrassing (as were many presentations) to w̶
_____s bad as the time the smart ass who always sat in the back̶
_____ss wearing a white karate outfit and who asked a kid nam̶
_____t the front of the class and raised his hand immediately
_____ked a question if he'd be interested in assisting him durin̶
_____ch the amenable Sam shrugged and said, "Sure," and sto̶
_____imself to be positioned in the middle of the room by this ̶
_____e the deceased has forgotten, but then the karate kid pulled ̶
_____ockets a red and white box of Marlboro Reds, from whi̶
_____ing it between the lips of this Sam kid, makin̶
_____ifying his inherent nerdiness and thus̶
_____n he normally looked, but the smar̶
_____n to do his work, which was essen̶
_____of his mastery of karate, and on̶
_____as transpiring here in the classro̶
_____e winced but ultimately thought
_____*e was a hundred percent sure he c̶*
_____h if the karate kid had been able̶
_____this particular occasion since ̶

River Teeth
Nonfiction Conference
Ashland University, Ashland, Ohio | May 30-June 1, 2014

Featuring Guest Speakers

Brenda Miller   Philip Gerard

and Writers and Editors

Jill Christman, Bob Cowser, Jr., Valerie Due,
Hope Edelman, Jill Gerard, Steven Harvey,
Kate Hopper, Sonya Huber, Dan Lehman,
Joe Mackall, Ana Maria Spagna, and Sarah M. Wells

Conference Emphasis on the Essay,
Memoir, and Literary Journalism
25-page OR Book-length Manuscript Consultations Available
Two Full Days of Panels, Seminars, and Readings

April 1 Priority Deadline for $50 Off Registration
www.riverteethjournal.com/conference | riverteeth@ashland.edu
401 College Avenue | Ashland, OH 44805 | 419.289.5957

 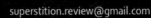

THE IOWA REVIEW

poem, story, essay, art
April, August, December

iowareview.org

LIBRARY RECOMMENDATION FORM

I would like to recommend the acquisition of *Fourth Genre: Explorations in Nonfiction* (ISSN 1094-8392), published two (2) times a year by Michigan State University Press.

PRINT SUBSCRIPTION PRICE (1 YEAR/2 ISSUES)

UNITED STATES INSTITUTIONS $126
INTERNATIONAL INSTITUTIONS $146

Institutional Electronic and Print & Electronic subscriptions available through *jstor.org*.

Thank you for your consideration of this request.

_____
NAME

_____
SIGNATURE

_____
EMAIL

_____
INSTITUTION

_____
DEPARTMENT

TO SUBSCRIBE: VISIT *www.msupress.org/journals/fg/*; EMAIL *msupjournals@cambeywest.com*; CALL (845) 267-3054; FAX (845) 267-3478; or SEND ORDERS AND INQUIRIES TO: Michigan State University Press; PO Box 121; Congers, NY 10920-0121.

— Copy, complete, and forward this form to your library —

fOURTH GENRe

2014 SUBSCRIPTION RATES (1 YEAR / 2 ISSUES)

UNITED STATES	INTERNATIONAL
Individual Print $42	Individual Print $62
Individual Electronic $38	Individual Electronic $38
Individual Print & Electronic $47	Individual Print & Electronic $69
Institutional Print $126	Institutional Print $146

Student Print or Electronic $26
Student Print & Electronic $47

Institutional Electronic and Print & Electronic subscriptions available through *jstor.org*.

PREPAYMENT REQUIRED: check, money order, Visa, and MasterCard accepted. Make checks payable to Michigan State University Press. Payment must be in U.S. currency drawn from a U.S. bank.

☐ Yes! I would like to subscribe to *Fourth Genre*.
☐ Please renew my subscription.

_____
NAME

_____
STREET ADDRESS

_____
CITY / STATE / ZIP

_____
TELEPHONE   FAX

_____
E-MAIL

☐ Payment enclosed, check made payble to *Michigan State University Press*.

☐ Please charge my: ☐ Visa   ☐ MasterCard

_____
CARD NUMBER (OR CALL 845/267-3054 FOR PRIVACY)   EXPIRATION DATE

_____
SIGNATURE   DATE

TO SUBSCRIBE: VISIT *www.msupress.org/journals/fg/*; EMAIL *msupjournals@ cambeywest.com*; CALL (845) 267-3054; FAX (845) 267-3478; or SEND ORDERS AND INQUIRIES TO: Michigan State University Press; PO Box 121; Congers, NY 10920-0121.